CELTIC SYMBOLS

THE ESSENTIAL GUIDE TO THEIR HISTORY, EVOLUTION, AND INFLUENCE ON ARTISTIC EXPRESSION

WITH 70 ILLUSTRATIONS, 40 IN COLOUR

BY

CLARE ELIZABETH BONNER

HADLEY PAGER INFO

First Edition 2007

ISBN 978-1-872739-18-2
(1-872739-18-0)

Copyright © Clare Elizabeth Bonner

All rights reserved including translation. This publication, or any part of it, may not be reproduced, stored in a retrieval system or transmitted in any form without the prior written permission of the publisher. The cover design is the copyright of Clare Elizabeth Bonner and Hadley Pager Info

Printed and bound by SC International Pte Ltd.,
Singapore

HADLEY PAGER INFO
Leatherhead, Surrey, England

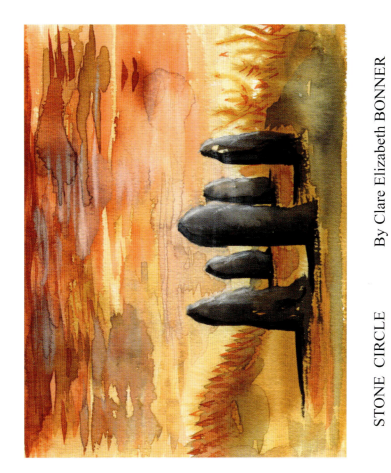

STONE CIRCLE By Clare Elizabeth BONNER

FOREWORD

The symbols, motifs and mythological characters described in this book are based on research collated from many different sources. Each account sourced has almost always subtly varied, and therefore the information contained on the following pages, is based on a general and overall consensus of historical records. Archaeologists and historians have discovered, researched and accounted for evidence, which enables us to have a greater insight into our antiquity. However, each country may have their own recorded historical account, which as I have mentioned earlier, can sometimes vary or be conflicting with other official findings. This means that names, the spelling of names and places are not necessarily represented in the same form, although the actual symbolism notably remains consistent. Over the passage of time, facts will undoubtedly alter as new discoveries are made or ancient historical records are proved inaccurate. The misspelling of Queen Boudicca's name, originally recorded as Bodicea, is an interesting example.

Much of the illustrative work is based on actual archaeological artefacts, which I have used to represent the various symbols described in the book. The definition of each source however, has sometimes been ambiguous and occasionally conflicting, therefore, I have represented the images and interpreted their possible significations accordingly.

C.E.B.

ACKNOWLEDGEMENT

Firstly, I would like to thank my husband Bruno and my two children, Fabien and Solène for the patience they have demonstrated, whilst I have been buried in books and reliving the worlds of ancient civilizations these past two years. I would also like to thank my good friend and proof-reader Shirley Sutton, who has been an endless source of inspiration and encouragement. Also Clive Caroll for his 'pearls of wisdom' many years ago when I was once part of his English class. And finally in memory of my father George Edgar Radford Bonner, who has been all of the above and so much more, and to whom I would like to dedicate this book.

Thank you to the various museums and libraries for their assistance in my research.

C.E.B.

CONTENTS

                                                                           PAGE

CHAPTER ONE

    The Celts   13
    The Origin and Spread of the Celts   16

CHAPTER TWO

    Celtic Symbols   23

        Apple Tree   24
        Ash Tree   25
        Bear   26
        Birds   27
        Boar, Pig   28
        Boat   30
        Bull   31
        Butterfly   32
        Cat   33
        Cauldron   34
        Circle   36
        Club   37
        Cockerel   38
        Colours   39
        Crane   41
        Cross   42
        Crow, Raven   44
        Dog, Hounds   45
        Dove   46
        Dragon   47

	PAGE
Eagle, Falcon, Hawk	48
Fertility	50
Fire	52
Griffon	54
Harp	56
Hazel Tree	57
Head	58
Heron	59
Horn	60
Horse	62
Lance	63
Lion, Leopard	64
Mistletoe	65
Numbers	66
Oak Tree	69
Owl	70
Patterns	71
Ram	73
Salmon	74
Snake, Serpent	76
Spirals	77
Stag, Deer	78
Stones	79
Swan	81
Swastika/Svastika	82
Sword	83
Torque	84
Tree	85
Trinity/Triad /Triangle	86
Triskele/Triskelion	88
Water	90
Wheel	92
Wolf	92
Wren	94
Yew Tree	94

	PAGE

CHAPTER THREE

    The Evolution of Celtic Symbolism   96

    The Evolution of Celtic Symbols   105

    Evolution of the

Cockerel	105
Cross	106
Dove	108
Dragon	110
Falcon and Hawk	111
Griffon	112
Harp	116
Lion	117
Owl	119
Salmon	121
Snake	123
Swastika	124
Triskele/Triskelion	126

GLOSSARY OF MYTHOLOGICAL CHARACTERS
AND CELTIC TERMS   129

BIBLIOGRAPHY   143
OTHER SOURCES OF INFORMATION   146
ILLUSTRATIONS: Sources and Acknowledgements   147

CHAPTER ONE

THE CELTS

Throughout the decades, much has been written about the Celts; from the ancient Greeks to the Romans, historical accounts have been recorded, giving us an insight into their distinctive and vibrant existence.

Herodotus, Strabo, Plato, Lucretius and Julius Caesar are but a few of the great names that we can associate today, with the earliest written references of these peoples. It must be remembered however, that Caesars' accounts of the Celts could be considered biased, as the Romans suffered countless defeats at the hands of these peoples, whom they regarded and described as barbaric tribes. Ancient historians have equally recorded that in fact the Greeks and the Romans, were both known to have recognised the Celts' wisdom and intelligence. With the introduction of Christianity, the monks also contributed to many of the historical accounts written about the Celts, although later evidence has revealed that not all that was recorded was necessarily accurate.

They were depicted as fearless warriors and were reputed to frequently fight naked or semi-clothed, adorned with jewellery such as the torque and equipped with elaborate armoury. Helmets worn by chiefs could be adorned with statuettes, such as birds like the eagle, or animals such as the boar. Many Pictish tribes were referred to by some ancient historians as 'Picture People', as they were known for painting their bodies before going into battle. The Celts were often used as mercenaries by other armies, and their fearsome appearance would strike fear into the hearts of their adversaries. Their tenacious nature, combined with the excellence and superior craftsmanship of their weaponry, only compounded their reputation.

Ancient historians have also described them as a fair and noble race, ruled by their Kings, Queens and chiefs, who governed their peoples under the power and guidance of the Druids, establishing their own aristocratic caste system. They lived peaceably amongst themselves in communities, farming the land and keeping livestock, as well as sharing a common pagan religion involving superstitious beliefs. It was these beliefs that spilled over into everyday life, until objects, animals, parts of the human form, as well as nature and especially the elements of nature, developed a symbolic importance. These were notably associated with Druidism, and combined with their mythology, certain symbols developed a greater significance than others in association with particular divinities. Sacrifices to these divinities were part of their culture and pagan religion, and each form and method of sacrifice was equally symbolic. Their rituals involving human sacrifices often portrayed them as heathens but in Celtic tradition death only signified an opening and a journey to the Otherworld where life continued. Sacrifices were also common in other cultures and it should not be forgotten that the Romans for example, actually made these into a sport.

Their culture and artistic influences developed through trading, and later with migrations, and they were often influenced by the art and symbolism of other cultures, such as those of the ancient Egyptians, the Etruscans, the Hittites, and the Greeks, sometimes sharing similar representation and meaning. Although inspired by other cultures, the Celts were however adept at producing a wealth of diverse art, which they developed into their own inimitable style. Following Romanisation and the eventual conversion to Christianity for many, the Celts found new forms of expression; although in general, the spiritual significance of their symbolism remained unchanged. They were inspired by nature and influenced by the earliest art forms of man, producing zoomorphic designs, spirals and circles as well as intricate knot-work. This resulted in elaborate and highly decorative art forms, which would later influence the early monasteries, becoming particularly distinctive in many of the illuminated manuscripts.

Although much has been learnt through extensive archaeological research and evidence, there is still much supposition surrounding the Celts, and some controversy concerning the accuracy of the proffered conclusions. But despite divergent opinion, our fascination for the Celts and the incredible myths and legends which encompass them, has remained ever popular. Their creative ingenuity as well as their love for poetry and music, have greatly contributed to our Celtic heritage, something that is still an integral part of many cultures today. The power of art as a medium of expression since man could draw his first shape in the dirt has conspired to producing a remarkable impact on the future of art itself. It has been a tool and a voice sending messages to distant places, and used by ancient civilizations, simple iconography has been able to influence the masses.

This book looks at some of the more significant symbols and motifs of the Celts, which formed an essential part of their culture. It concludes by briefly illustrating their evolution and influence on art, design and literature from the Middle Ages to the twentieth century.

THE ORIGIN AND SPREAD OF THE CELTS

According to Herodotus, the Celts dwelt beyond the ' Pillars of Hercules' (the straits of Gibraltar) and that the Danube rose in their territory. He also claimed that they were one of the most westerly peoples of Europe. Ephorus wrote that along with the Persians, Scythians and Libyans, they could be included as one of the four most barbaric peoples of the known world. Herodotus and Ephorus were referring to the tribes of peoples, known as the Celts. The Greek merchants referred to them as Keltoi or Galatae, distinctive linguistically and sharing many common characteristics, including their appearance, religious beliefs and their political and social structure.

It was from the sixth century BC, that the earliest Greek writings appeared, documenting the first real evidence of these peoples. The Greeks were known to refer to them for their knowledge and wisdom in subjects such as geography, philosophy and astronomy, attributes which the Romans also valued, demonstrated by their use of Celtic tutors in the education of their sons. Trading formed an important part of their development and culture, which flourished between the Mediterranean Celts from the west, the Greeks, the Phoenicians and the Etruscans.

Descending from the Bronze Age, Tumulus and Urnfield cultures, an important and distinctive civilisation emerged in Hallstatt in Middle-Europe between 1200 BC and 475 BC. The Hallstatt culture as it became known, was an iron-using and salt-mining economy in the Austrian Salzkammergut. This culture seemingly overlapped the 'proto-Celtic' Urnfield period, named after their custom of burying their dead in flat cemeteries following cremation, and placing the remains in urns.

Archaeological findings at Lake Hallstatt, uncovered evidence of princely tombs containing wagons and iron swords, with ornamented hilts and sheaths as well as geometrically patterned pottery and other decorative artefacts including gold ornaments. Examples of Phoenician glass and amber from the Baltic were also identified, indicative of their connection with trade and commerce. It was these connections through trading, which influenced and enhanced many of the creative aspects of their culture, providing them with valuable sources of inspiration.

With the emergence of the La Tène culture at the north-eastern end of Lake Neuchatel, Switzerland, from the fifth to first century BC, the Celts were now at their height of development and expansion. With inventive and more sophisticated methods of transport and farming, living standards improved considerably, encouraging settlements to grow whilst remaining self-sufficient. Their increasing skills enabled them to produce more advanced pieces of pottery and other objects, which were often unique and highly decorative, involving spirals, curves and bosses, combined with influences from Graeco-Etruscan art. They were also the first in producing enamelled work, and their craftsmanship and advanced techniques in metalwork swiftly established their weaponry as superior to that of neighbouring tribes. These remarkable and innovative skills contributed greatly in establishing the recognition of the importance of their civilization and culture in Europe.

From the seventh century BC, spreading from their homeland, north of the Alps, the Celts settled in the Po valley, defeating the Estruscan armies, followed later by the Sennones defeat of Rome in 390 BC. Led by Brennus, they occupied the Capitol for seven months, before withdrawing victoriously for a sum of gold. Their widespread migration continued, spreading westward into France and Iberia, southward into Italy and eastwards to the Balkans, reaching as far as the Black Sea, and spreading southwards towards Delphi, which they sacked in 279 BC, before penetrating Asia Minor.

Renowned warriors and feared by the other Europeans, the Celts were frequently recruited as mercenaries, fighting for the Greeks, Egyptians, the Syracuse and eventually the Carthaginians, commanded by Antaros during their conflict against Rome. Ancient historians recorded that fifty percent of Hannibal's army consisted of Celts from the Alpine

Region, who assisted in his crossing into the Po Valley; and that during 218 BC to 201 BC they played an important part in his Italian campaigns. But by the second and first centuries BC, with the Roman Empire spreading its tentacles into new provinces, Celtic territories found themselves subjugated by this dominant force; and coupled with the pressures from Germanic and Slavic tribes and their own weakening lack of cohesion, the Celtic stronghold was soon in decline. Dissension continued through mid-Europe until eventually only Gaul retained almost any form of Celtic law and leadership, the British Islands still remaining free from Romanisation. However, despite intensive resistance against the Roman armies, Gaul too was finally conquered during the fall of Alesia with the defeat of the Celtic chief, Vercingetorix; who having surrendered himself to Caesar, spent several years in imprisonment until his eventual execution in Rome.

Although the Celts did not invade the British Islands, subsequent to the growing pressures from other tribes and the Roman expansion, there was a steady infiltration of these groups of peoples from Europe into Britain and Ireland; which increased during 100 BC and 100 AD. Many of the Belgae, during the first century BC, had already migrated to southern Britain. These migrations brought with them the spread of the Celtic language and new elements from other civilizations, influences from the Urnfield and La Tène cultures were evident, especially in southern and eastern Britain. Sharing certain common characteristics and with the introduction of new iron tools, farming continued to develop, becoming an important and integral part of their civilization. Ritual worship, sacrifices and votive offerings to the divinities acquired an even greater importance, being associated with the seasonal changes and cultivating the earth. Sowing and harvesting became linked to fertility as well as the sun and the moon, and were celebrated by thanking the Gods. Britain at this time had forged its own strong and distinctive culture and artistic style, which was well established before its eventual Romanisation.

It was through trade that the earliest written references to Britain and Ireland appeared, when in the sixth century BC, a voyage known as the 'Massiliote Periplus' was undertaken from Massilia, and referred to two large islands, Albion and Ierne. Pytheas of Massilia, the Greek explorer, later refers to them as the Pretanic Islands, however it was the geographer Eratosthenes of Cyrene who correctly placed Ireland on the map around 300 BC.

Soon it was Britain's turn to yield to the force of the Romans. After exploratory visits made by Caesar in 55 and 54 BC, the great Roman invasion of Britain followed in AD 43, led by Aulus Plautius, Claudius's commander and newly appointed governor of Britain. Despite defeating the Britons, the Romans' overall domination of Britain was never complete as Scotland managed to stay free from Roman rule, regardless of their attempts to conquer its barbarian territories. Whilst certain tribes assimilated well, many Celts fled to the north; Cornwall and Devon were able to maintain many of their Celtic traditions and certain more remote areas of Wales were also less affected. Only Ireland and Scotland remained untouched.

However, the rebellions increased, and in AD 61, Boudicca led the Iceni tribe in a widespread attack against the Romans.

Despite having lived compatibly amongst the Romans as their allies and enjoying a similar lifestyle, the Romans in reality harboured much resentment towards Boudicca and the power she held with the Druids, whom they considered a threat. Following the death of her husband King Prasutagus, the Romans publicly flogged the Iceni Queen as well as raping her daughters, and the humiliation fuelled the anger and hatred of her peoples, who joined Boudicca in seeking revenge. Tens of thousands fought with her in one of history's most significant attacks on the Romans, as she first sacked Colchester, followed by London and St Albans. However, their heroic flaming-haired Queen was finally defeated by the Roman legions. They then exacted a terrible revenge against the Iceni tribes, massacreing whole villages, including women and children. Having failed to destroy the Romans and witnessing the horrific slaughter of her own peoples, Boudicca reputedly took her life, by swallowing poison.

The Romanisation of Britain continued and with the conversion of Emperor Constantine to Christianity, the Celts also began converting to this new religion, relinquishing many of their traditions and superstitious beliefs. But regardless of the Romans' attempt at a peaceable rule, the conflicts increased and with invasions from the Picts, Scoti and Irish, and pillaging by the Franks and Saxons, their provinces were under perpetual threat.

By AD 410, the Romans withdrew from Britain, under the command of the Emperor Honorius, leaving the island fragmented into small kingdoms. Vulnerable and no longer under Roman protection, Britain was once again assailed by the Saxons, Angles and Jutes; in search of fertile land, the

Angles and Saxons laid claim to new territories in the South. Defiant and unwilling to submit to these incursions, the Celts in retaliation managed to defeat these Germanic invaders in the Battle of Badon in AD 493; however despite their victory, Britain remained in a volatile state. With growing friction, further battles ensued, culminating in the mass migration of Celtic tribes, fleeing to Cornwall, Wales, Ireland as well as the Isle of Man and the peninsular of Armorica (Brittany), whilst many others who remained were massacred.

The Anglo-Saxon territories eventually became known as England and with the introduction of different cultural influences, most of the ancient Celtic traditions gradually disappeared. Cornwall, Wales and Brittany however, retained much of their Celtic identity, sharing a common folkloric culture with Scotland and Ireland, which had remained unscathed by conflict and subjugation; therefore allowing them to truly preserve their Celtic heritage and independence.

CHAPTER TWO

CELTIC SYMBOLS

The following symbols and motifs have been selected primarily because they are the ones that have been consistently represented in Celtic tradition. Their association and relationship with the numerous deities and other spiritual aspects of Celtic society mentioned in the book, also suggest, that the Celts possibly regarded them as some of the more significant emblems within their culture.

# pple Tree

The apple tree shared a particular importance with the oak and was one of the more significant trees in Celtic tradition. Like the oak, it was also linked to the Otherworld, its fruit, regarded to be the fruit of science possessing special magical qualities, symbolizing revelation as well as immortality. In Irish legend, Maelduin, went in search of the assassin of his father, and joined by seventeen men, they set off in a boat but found that they had to circumnavigate several treacherous islands. One of these islands however, offered them sustenance, and on another they nourished on the apples of immortality for forty days. In mythology, those who eat an apple will not want and so will no longer feel thirst, nor hunger. It was also believed to be the fruit of wisdom, and in Celtic legend, Merlin taught under an apple tree. The mystic place known as Avalon was also referred to as Apple Island and was Arthur's final resting place. There he was cared for and watched over by Morgane as he fell into a deep sleep after being gravely injured. In mythology, the apple has also been associated with fertility, temptation and peace.

sh Tree

In Ireland, it was the ash that was considered to be one of the most important and sacred of trees, along with the oak and the yew, and in ancient Gaul it represented strength and immortality. This attractive forest tree was known for its hard and resilient white wood and was associated with fire, producing a fine white ash when burnt. Its branches were also used for burning during the winter solstice. Certain traditional expressions mention the ash or ashes, when they refer to something or someone looking ashen or ashy.

Bear

Once a royal emblem for kingdoms such as Persia and Russia, the bear represented immense strength and associated with the aspects of war it was symbolic of the great warriors. Attributed to Artio, the goddess of bears, whose image also personified the cruelness of death, certain important heroes took their name from this goddess, and bear-cults were established primarily for its worship. In Celtic legend, the first three letters ART, which derive from Artio are evident in these names, the most recognisable being Arthur. In Celtic mythology, the boar also represented Druidism and magic, and opposed the bear, represented as Arthur's soldier, in the struggle for spiritual sovereignty, which is recounted in the story of Arthur's fantastic and ceaseless chase of a monstrous white sow, Twrch Trwyth, which evades him. The symbols of bears and boars were later engraved in places of religious worship during the evolution of the Roman influence. The constellation, The Great Bear, has also been referred to as Arthur's chariot and in heraldry, this great and ferocious creature is often depicted muzzled.

Birds

In Celtic tradition, birds held many different symbolic values and were generally associated with the Otherworld. In Welsh mythology, the goddess Rhiannon takes the souls of mortals to the otherworld and possesses many magical birds, which can enchant the living to sleep and equally awaken the dead, bringing joy or forgetfulness that can last for seven years. Morrigann, a goddess associated with love and death as well as warfare, is able to take the form of the crow when attributed to battle, or is depicted in triple form as three crows or rooks, representing eternity. Deities associated with the sky could assume the appearance of a bird such as Oenghus when he transforms himself into a swan or Lleu who changes into an eagle upon his death. The eagle was associated with fire and air, the heron with water and the crow with death, and represented many of the aspects, which were spiritually symbolic in Celtic society.

Certain birds were also associated with divine powers and strength as well as being prophetic or wise and were sometimes believed to be messengers or carriers of souls, to and from the Otherworld, such as the blackbird. These were usually favoured by the druids and included the wren, the owl and the crow or raven. Others such as the dove or the peacock, a solar bird like the cockerel and the eagle, were symbolic of purity and immortality, or like the wren, symbolic of good fortune and prosperity.

Boar / Pig

Representing strength and aggression, venerated for its tenacity, the boar was commonly associated with battle; distinguished for its ferocious and fearless nature, unafraid to face its enemy, it became emblematic in war, particularly with the Gauls.

The boar was frequently depicted in statue form or on coins, brooches and helmets, with its dorsal bristles raised in hostility, and references to its bristles have appeared in various epics, signifying that they were also perhaps considered symbolic. This primeval animal was much prized by the hunter and was often depicted with certain deities attributed to the animals of the forest. Ardiunna, the Goddess associated with hunting, was portrayed astride a boar, dagger in hand.

Associated with other Gods such as Lug, it was also symbolic of the Otherworld, a spiritual power and provider, with its meat highly ritualized at the feasts of the deities. The boar was also regarded for its knowledge, as it fed on the fruits of trees such as the oak, which were sacred to the druids, bonding it as well to the mysteries of the forest.

The pig, especially the sow, was also esteemed for its wisdom and symbolized healing, health and festivity. It was also considered an important animal in the Otherworld.

Boat

The boat was symbolic in Celtic tradition, and the ancient Celtic vessels were covered in skin, resembling the coracles, which are still used in Ireland and Wales today. Associated with the journey to the Otherworld, 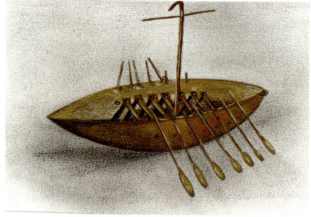 the boat represented a safe passage, and in Irish legend, Manannan Mac Liv, their sea god, carried away mythical heroes in a boat beneath the waves. It could also represent punishment, as Celtic tradition demanded that criminals could be exiled by boat, set adrift without any means of paddling or steerage.

The boat also possessed other symbolic meanings, and examples of model boats have been found, suggesting a votive significance. A fine example is the golden boat from Broighter in county Derry, Ireland, where its seven oars are reputed to represent the seven orifices of the human body. Its form has also appeared in carvings such as the one found on the bronze solar wheel, discovered in Charroux, France, indicating a link with the sun and the solar deities.

Bull

Symbolizing strength, the bull in its feral form, representing untamed power, was revered by the Celts. When tamed by man, it was associated with domesticity and wealth, providing families with a means for living, as well as being used for bartering. Stealing cattle was not uncommon, and the Irish legend, 'The Cattle Raid of Cooley' (Cualnge) recounts the tale of the attempted theft of a valuable brown bull.

This ancient symbol, also represented sovereignty and was considered sacrificial, in particular, before the crowning of a new king. In ancient Ireland, 'the feast of the bull' (tabhfheis) took place before a ceremony such as this. Cernunnos has sometimes been depicted with the horns of a bull, symbolizing fertility and renewal. In mythology, the bull could also be represented with three horns. The bull and its bovine counterparts have appeared in varying symbolic forms as engravings or on helmets and as statues, more commonly in bronze.

Associated with other Gods such as Esus and Lug, it was also symbolic of the Otherworld, a spiritual power and provider, with its meat highly ritualized at the feasts of the deities.

Butterfly

The butterfly has appeared in different cultures and traditions including that of the Celts. It represented the souls of the dead in the Otherworld, as the soul was believed to be able to transform itself into another entity.

It was considered positive as opposed to negative and was symbolic of freedom. In some ancient civilizations, the moth could replace the butterfly, however its symbolism could equally represent the darker aspects of the Otherworld.

Cat

The real significance of the cat in Celtic tradition is uncertain, although in mythology there have been numerous references to them. They often appeared as guardians, and in the epic of Bricrui, Cuchulainn resists the three Druidic cats that await him at the dwelling of Medb. They could also appear as guardians in the Otherworld and were generally seen as shape-shifters, symbolic of goddesses, especially those attributed to lunar worship, their eyes being symbolic perhaps of the crescent moon and their ability to see in the dark; they were equally associated with druids, witches and magic.

In Gaul, Ireland, and to certain Pictish tribes, the cat was regarded with greater importance, whereas in other cultures such as ancient Egypt, the cat was revered and considered sacred. The Roman goddess of liberty was represented with a cup in one hand, a sceptre in the other and a cat lying at her feet; and its image has been depicted on objects such as the bronze mirror of Holcombe, Devon or the cross of Muiredach, Monasterboice, Co. Louth, Ireland. The cat is also reputed to possess nine lives.

Cauldron

This ancient and multi-faceted object was largely symbolic of death and resurrection, offering spiritual knowledge, healing and immortality, as well as the power to intoxicate. Symbolic also of fire and water, the cauldron was an essential element to the ritual ceremonies of the Otherworld, its feasting and rebirth. It was believed that after placing the dead in this sacred vessel, within the following days they would be reborn. The most celebrated of these myths recounts the story of Bran, master of life and death, who possessed a divine cauldron.

Many legends have depicted magical cauldrons, providing an eternal supply of sustenance and have been associated with deities such as Dagda, who replenished tired troops with an endless supply of nourishment, thereby symbolizing abundance and regeneration.

Apart from its spiritual qualities, the cauldron was fundamental in its domestic capacity of providing food and storage, and was an integral part of family and village life, representing not only beliefs but also survival. The Gundestrup cauldron is probably one of the finest surviving examples today of this type of vessel.

Circle

Like the wheel, the circle also has powerful religious connotations. Megalithic sites such as Avebury and Stonehenge are prime examples of the ritual pagan worship of the sun and moon practised in druidic ceremonies.

Geoffrey of Monmouth recounted that it was Merlin who brought the huge stone blocks that form Stonehenge all the way from Ireland and that they had formerly originated from Africa after being brought to Ireland by giant magicians. These ancient circular temples signified a sacred enclosure or sanctuary, symbolizing a celestial and magical centre and space. Its cosmic and metaphysical importance can be identified in the Druids' cross, which although consisting of eight circles, is in essence the three concentric circles, Keugant, Abred and Gwenwed, which form its principle elements. The dimensions of the circle Gwenwed have been used for the basis of other measurements of a number of megalithic sites. Fortifications were usually built in circle form such as the ring-forts at the ancient site of Tara, in Co.unty Meath, a sacred hill-site, which was once the seat of the Kings of Ireland.

The circle appears consistently in Celtic symbolism and art, represented in varying formations, on the ground, in stone, as well as jewellery such as brooches.

 lub

The club, also known as a cudgel, was a weapon associated with warfare and was therefore symbolic to the Celts, representing power, strength and even in some contexts, virility, and like certain other weaponry, it was often attributed to heroes.

In mythology, Daghda, the druid-god, possesses three magical objects: a harp, a cauldron and a club made from a yew tree. The club associated with warfare, had the power to kill with one end or equally restore life with the other. Daghda was the father of the living and master of the dead. In heraldry, the club is symbolic of guardianship.

Cockerel

Associated with the sunrise, and attributed to Hermes, the god of light, this solar bird represented the lust for life and vigilance, its morning call announcing the beginning of a new day and the continuance of life with the arrival of dawn. Amongst certain other symbols, the cockerel represented guardianship, watching over the ancient power of expression as well as appearing on church spires, where it confronted the elements, defending and remaining vigilant over its domain. Even today, the cockerel is still found on weather vanes.

It was also a holy bird and was associated with ancient Druidism, and has been linked to fertility. Its image has been engraved on stones, symbolizing eternity, and although mainly portrayed in a positive light, it has also been depicted in certain places of worship in relation to the anti-Christ, with a serpent's tail, signifying a dark and malevolent aspect.

According to ancient mythology it was the white cockerel, which appeared on coinage from Gaul, which was the name given to France during the time of the Roman occupation. 'Gallus' is also the Latin name for cockerel, not dissimilar to the word Gaul. Later, the cockerel in general became emblematic to France with the spread of the Franks.

# Colours

The Celts were fascinated not only with patterns and shapes but also with colour, which they used creatively in their artwork. Their clothing and jewellery also expressed their bold and colourful nature. Some of the remnants of clothing found by archaeologists are not in fact dissimilar to the design of tartan. They were also known to use colours to guide them and referred to them as points of reference concerning the four directions. There were however certain colours which were considered more symbolic than others, such as **red**, which was generally associated with the Otherworld or underworld. Many references to this colour can be found in Celtic mythology, attributed to warfare, the deities of war and the dead. The retinue of Morrigann, the triple goddess was red and it has also been used in the name or title of a character, such as Aed Ruad, one of the three kings in Irish legend, who was also referred to as Aed-the-Red, father of Macha-the-Redhead. The colour red was considered symbolic of beauty, perhaps because many of the Celts were red-headed.

Blue was associated with productivity and the functions of the artisan and was a colour especially symbolic to the Picts, who utilized it predominately as one of the numerous colours that they painted on their bodies. It is also a colour, like that of green, which is representative of the elements, the sky, the sea and all that consists of nature itself.

The colour **white** is one notably associated with the druids and their functions as well as also being attributed to kings and poets. In Celtic tradition, white was symbolic of the light, but it was also representative of purity and is a colour still associated with religion. In Wales, the signification of white represented happiness, in Gaul it represented beauty and in Ireland, saintliness. Like the colour red, there have also been many references to white in Celtic mythology; the wild and monstrous sow, Twrch Trwyth, which Arthur chases is white, symbolic of spiritual sovereignty, and the white sow, Twrch Henwen, as depicted in Welsh legend, represents the forces of all that is spiritual. One of the many names of the supreme god, Lug, was that of 'Lug with the White Hand'.

Crane

The mysteries of the crane remain ambiguous. Associated with water and transformation, when portrayed in Celtic mythology, heroic characters have been seemingly changed into the form of a crane. This apparent transformation was often synonymous with punishment or deception.

Manannan, son of the ocean and lord of the other world, foreshadowed Fionn and Cuchulainn by bringing the secret treasures of the sea in a bag made from the skin of a crane. With its warrior connotations, the crane was also symbolic in battle, representing life and death. With the ability to possess the strength of the enemy, like the crow, it could be considered as a bad omen and it has been depicted on various types of weaponry.

Cross

Some of the earliest images of the cross were commonly depicted in a circle with a central point and were essentially symbolic to the druids in the ritual pagan worship of the sun. The circle represented the sun and the light, and the cross within it represented the four directions of the seasons, the elements and the divine forces of the cosmos. The centre of this cross symbolized its central power, where all becomes one, the origin of the beginning of life itself, and so it was therefore also regarded as the cross of life, later becoming known as the Celtic cross. Its centre was sometimes depicted with a motif similar to that of the swastika or the triskele and the cross of Saint Brigitte in Ireland is a fine example of this representation.

Throughout early pagan worship, the cross remained symbolic

of religion and its image has been depicted on a number of megalithic monuments as well as on pottery and on coinage, such as examples found in Gaul. Certain megalithic sites were also built in the form of a cross, such as the tumulus at New Grange or the site of Calanais off the coast of Scotland. During the iron and bronze ages, many crosses included other symbolic imagery, including animals and numeric references; and with the introduction of Christianity, crosses appeared depicting biblical scenes and saints. In Ireland a large number of stone crosses were produced in varying forms and sizes; and in places such as the Isle of Man and Wales, the wheel cross, which was also associated with the tree of life, was more commonly found.

Crow / Raven

The crow, like the raven, was considered a wise and prophetic bird, possessing divine qualities. It was often an infallible guide to ancient navigators, but also symbolic, as was the raven, of guiding those on their journey into the Otherworld. The crow was also attributed to the deities, and the great crow was emblematic to the supreme God Lug, and in Celtic legend, Bran was also known as 'Bran the Crow'. It represented healing and light, but as well, a certain mystery and magic, concealing darker and hidden depths, and like the raven, was associated with druids and witchcraft. In Celtic mythology they were also both symbolic of warfare and death. Macha and Badbh, Goddesses of war, were able to transform themselves into the form of a crow, which when sighted by the warriors before battle, was considered as an ominous sign.

Dog / Hounds

Guardian and protector of this world and the Otherworld, the dog was also a hunter, associated with mythical heroes of war and in this context was not necessarily viewed with a positive image, appearing particularly noxious after the introduction of Christianity. Arawn, who presided over the kingdom of the dead, was master of a pack of white hounds with red ears, representing souls of the Otherworld.

The dog however, was also regarded as an adaptable creature, respected for its loyalty and companionship to man, and it reputedly possessed the power to heal through its saliva. The druids believed that the dog guarded the secrets of the Otherworld and that by chewing its flesh, it would empower them to divine the future.

Cu Chulainn, known also in ancient mythology as Setanta, was the most legendary of mythical Irish heroes; but after killing the hound of Caulann, the smith, he took the name of Cu Chulainn, 'The dog of Cualann', and was forbidden to kill a dog or eat its meat.

Dove

The dove has always been recognised as symbolic of peace and perhaps more notably when associated with the olive branch, peace and hope, as depicted in the story of Noah. It was often a messenger and also sometimes perceived as an oracular bird.

In some cultures doves were associated with the renewal of life, and were the denizens of the heavens, attributed to certain female deities of love and fertility, therefore linking them to Mother Earth. It was also believed that they were so pure and divine, that they could not be poisoned, and in ancient Celtic civilization the dove was considered to possess curative properties, its image symbolic to the healing gods. With the introduction of Christianity, the dove became symbolic with the baptism of Christ, becoming representative of the Holy Ghost, as frequently depicted in religious paintings throughout the centuries. The purity of the white dove also made it appropriate as a sacrificial offering for purification, and it was also believed that the dove, due to its purity, was the only creature that Satan was unable to take the form of. One of the earliest representations found of this bird, is a terracotta dove, discovered in Mesopotamia dating around 4500 BC.

Dragon

The dragon has been depicted in various guises, often synonymous with the serpent, which according to Celtic folklore can transform itself into a monster resembling the appearance of a dragon. Early depictions of the dragon are characteristic of the serpent. Associated with the powerful elements of earth, the dragon is a magical beast, symbolic of energy and force, and was also the guardian of treasures. This fire-breathing creature also appeared in emblematic form on the 'draco', the standards carried by the Roman legions during their invasion of Britain.

In the Arthurian legends, the red dragon was symbolic of the independence of the Welsh people and battled with the white dragon, which represented the Saxons, in their struggle for power. The dragon has continued to remain symbolic throughout history, and is today more commonly associated with the Welsh, when it appeared again in 1807 on the royal badge of Wales and was later adopted as their national symbol, officially recognised by the Queen in 1959.

Eagle, Falcon, Hawk

The noble and majestic eagle was considered a prophetic bird, which symbolized strength and wisdom as well as personifying air and fire. It was believed to have the power to fly towards the sun, and was therefore associated with the Celtic Sun God; however it was also symbolic to the Roman deity Jupiter, God of the skies. The eagle represent-ed companionship to the deities, was affiliated with the Goddess Dana, and was also linked to death, possessing spiritual qualities it had the ability to transport the soul to heaven. Lleu, upon his death, transformed himself into the form of an eagle, vanishing into the sky. Other birds of prey such as the **falcon** and the **hawk** were also associated with warriors and hunting, and were regarded, as was the eagle, as a prize. The eagle, in its imperial form, was emblematic, ornamenting the helmets of chieftains as well as frequently appearing with both the falcon and the hawk in heraldry. The image of the eagle was also depicted on coinage.

Eagle, Falcon, Hawk

Fertility

Fertility and all that it was associated with, has preoccupied cultures since the beginning of time, and civilizations have found different ways to express creatively their beliefs through diverse forms of symbolism. The association of fecundity and the mother-goddess or triple-goddess was predominant and their images were often depicted with other symbols of plenitude, usually represented in the form of certain foods. These divinities were notably depicted near water, usually a sacred source, such as the deity Sulis. The image of Sheela-na-gigs, the Celtic goddess of creation and destruction, is especially potent and is evocative of her strong sexual nature bound to the male fantasy.

If the vulva was symbolic, then the phallus was equally regarded as a potent symbol of fertility, and in Celtic tradition certain male divinities could be represented with an oversized and erect phallus, expressing their strength and sexual vigour. Gods such as Dagda was reputed to have an overly large penis, which he left uncovered or could drag along the ground. He too was attributed to fertility and the protection of the land. Reputed to possess great sexual prowess, he coupled with many of the fertility goddesses to ensure the continuation of earth's abundance.

It is believed that phallic cults existed and that the giant image carved into the hillside of Cerne Abbas in Dorset is undoubtedly the largest example of sexual expression and fertility. In ancient tradition, it was thought that couples copulating on the area of the giant's phallus were more likely to conceive. Whether the giant represented a particular deity is uncertain but it is possibly attributed to the god Hercules.

Other aspects of fertility were associated not only with conception but also with birth and rebirth. In mythology, many of the characters and heroes could be reborn several times, appearing under a different guise and name. Many were shape-shifters and could transform themselves into animals or other small things. In one epic, Keridwen (Kerridwen) in pursuit of Gwyon Bach transforms herself into a chicken and he into a grain of wheat, which she then swallows. Keridwen becomes pregnant and later gives birth to a son who she throws into the sea after placing him in a bag. The bag was later found by Elfinn a fisherman, who adopted the child and named him Taliesin.

Certain animals were also attributed to fertility, representing vitality and renewal. Cattle, but particularly the bull were significant, as was the ram, the boar, the pig and the horse, which was especially symbolic of sexual exuberance. Many of these animals were associated with particular deities and were therefore often depicted with their image.

Fire

Fire was an important source of heat and light in the Celtic civilization but like water, it also possessed a deeper symbolic significance. The ritual fire of Samhain, which burned between the thirty-first of October and the first of November, known as 'All Souls Day', marked the end of one year and the beginning of another. It not only represented protection but it was also a time to communicate with the dead. The second ritual fire of the Celtic calendar year was Beltain, associated with the god Belenos, who symbolized amongst other things, light, medicine and harmony. Held on the first of May, it represented the beginning of a second season, one of new life, light and a time of labour, when the Druids would drive the tribe's cattle between two fires for purification and to ward off evil. The Druids were essentially the masters of ritual fires, and it was not uncommon to sacrifice animals as well as humans to the deities as votive offerings. According to Roman historians, the victims were sometimes placed in wicker cages and set alight. Strabo, the Greek philosopher recorded that they constructed large sacrificial pyres.

In ancient Celtic tradition we know from the Urn culture, that their dead were cremated and placed in urns before burial, and that blacksmiths were regarded as superior because they produced exceptional objects and weaponry from fire. The cauldron, particularly significant to the Celts with its purifying and rejuvenating properties, may also have been linked to the symbolism of fire.

Fire

Griffon

This imaginary creature was one of ancient history's mythical and magical beasts and can be traced as far back as the Phoenicians. The most notable representation of the griffon is that consisting of a lion's hindquarters, with the talons, wings and usually the head of an eagle, but it was also sometimes depicted with a horse's or donkey's ears. The male griffon was sometimes depicted with raised spikes projecting from the neck in place of wings, but these representations began to appear less commonly. The griffon represented the strength

Wingless Griffon
From 7th Century BC Vase

and courage of the lion but equally possessed the rapidity and intelligence of the eagle. It was symbolic of guardianship and in Greek mythology it was the guardian of divine treasures.

It was also associated with the sun, and in early iconography it could appear pulling the sun chariot. Associated with the falcon, it was also symbolic of the feast of Beltane, held on the first of May in honour of the god Belenos, which in Celtic tradition was the day when the warmth of the sun and its light was welcomed at the beginning of a new season.

The griffon however could also be fierce and destructive, a killer of other animals and a renowned enemy of the horse. Its image was sometimes portrayed with that of the dragon, which it could also replace, or it could equally be portrayed with a serpent's tail. Depictions of the griffon have appeared in different forms of ancient art, and on pottery, greatly inspired by the Greeks, as well as being featured on coins and engraved on other objects such as the Gundestrup Cauldron.

Harp

The bard was a distinguished figure in Celtic society, a person of high status, of whom the most eminent possessed a harp particular to him, usually finely crafted and elaborately ornamented. The harp was considered a noble and divine instrument, endowed with magical properties, symbolizing the immortal soul. In ancient mythology, the god Dagda possessed a golden harp, which only played three melodies: laughter, sadness and eternal sleep. Lug, supreme god to the Celts, also possessed a magic harp with the same attributes but only his alone was able to play all melodies.

In Gaul it was the lyre, which was of greater significance and its image has been depicted on many ancient coins as well as appearing in other representations. In Wales the harp is still an important instrument and in Ireland it has become a national emblem, appearing on coins, flags and also on official buildings.

 azel Tree

The hazel tree was perhaps most noted for its fruit, the hazel nut, which was associated with knowledge and wisdom. In Celtic legend it is the salmon, which ate the nine nuts of wisdom and knowledge that fell from the hazel tree into the primeval spring of life beside it. In Celtic tradition the salmon is recognised for its wisdom and as a creature of science. As well as being associated with the salmon, the utilization of hazel wood, like that of the yew, has also been associated with the sacred writing of ogham. The branch from a hazel tree is believed to be able to divine the source of water.

Head

The human head was regarded as an omnipotent symbol and the decapitation of the enemy's head during and after battle was very symbolic. The ancient Celts believed that their enemy still had the power to cause them harm even after death and that by removing the victim's head, they would possess all their strength and wisdom. The decapitated head was considered a trophy and it was often hung from saddles or placed above doors. In Irish mythology, Cuchulainn hung the heads of his enemies from his chariot. The Celts were reputed to have kept them as a reminder of past victories, preserving them in cedar oil and sometimes removing the brain, which they mixed with lime rendering it hard, and this was also regarded as a trophy. As possessor of the soul, the head was considered sacred, and skulls were commonly placed above the entrances of sites of worship, and they were also used as sacrificial vessels. Many skulls, which archaeologists believe date from the Celtic period, have been discovered in the River Thames and are thought to have had a probable hallowed significance.

The head has been represented in many diverse forms, appearing on coins or as statues, as well as carvings and masks, and has also been portrayed as a double or triple head.

Heron

Birds associated with water were especially symbolic in Celtic tradition and numerous references can be found in Celtic mythology to water birds, such as the heron. They were symbolic of contemplation and divine wisdom and in mythology, Tarvos Trigaranos, the bull with three herons, symbolized the joining of divine knowledge with the  forces of earth. The castle of Arawn, lord of the kingdom of the dead was guarded by three herons, which prevented travellers from approaching with their cries of warning. Herons could also be associated with the mother goddess attributed to the creative forces of nature. These quiet and elegant birds with their long beaks and stilt-like legs are known to mate for life, which perhaps represented a stability and spiritual harmony in Celtic society. Their image like that of other water birds such as the goose, the swan and the crane, has been depicted on various objects, such as jewellery, armoury and different types of ornamentation, often interlaced with other motifs.

Horn

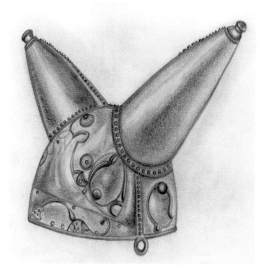

In Celtic tradition horned animals notably represented vitality, strength and often fertility, and their images were frequently depicted with the deities. Gods themselves could be represented with horns, such as Taranis, sometimes portrayed with three horns, or Tarvos (Taruos) the bull god, whose three cranes when symbolic of the three lunar phases, became three horns. Cernunnos, the 'horned god' was widely represented with other horned animals such as the stag, as well as the ram-headed serpent, both representing renewal and fertility. Images of horned gods similar to those of Cernunnos, have been found depicted on various altar stones, including those of Reims and Bourgogne in France.

Representations sometimes portrayed deities with the 'cornucopia' symbolic of plenty and also fertility, and in this context could therefore be attributed to the abundance of earth and the harvest. The goddess Epona was notably depicted with the 'horn of plenty' as was the Roman god Bacchus, who was also associated with the ram. The presence of horned animals during ritual ceremonies celebrating harvest time was not uncommon, and drinking from the horn itself became equally symbolic.

The horn also possessed warrior connotations, and attributed to animals such as the ram, the boar or the bull, it thus represented incredible strength and courage. Horned helmets were symbolic, and worn by the warrior-chiefs could signify not only their status, but also an association with the gods and their divine power.

Horse

Since the beginning of early Celtic civilization, the horse remained an important and integral element within their society. Initially regarded as a domestic animal, as were cattle and pigs, the horse was kept for both its meat and for transporting goods. With the spread of conflicts and war, the horse gained greater significance; revered by warriors, it represented  status and nobility to those that rode into battle either on its back or by chariot; these were often highly embellished, as was the horse's bridle. The horse also symbolized beauty, speed and sexual exuberance, the embodiment of power and energy, with the mare synonymous of life in motion. Associated also with water and healing, it was emblematic to several divinities, including that of the warrior. The mare was more commonly attributed to the great war-goddess Epona, who assured the safe passage of the souls of the deceased to the otherworld.

A solar sign, the horse also possessed certain sacred and religious denotations, which have been represented in various statues and effigies. It has also been portrayed in a hybrid form with a human head or with wings and has appeared on many ancient coins. Horse-remains, along with other livestock, have been uncovered in numerous burial sites, often accompanied with chariots or wagons.

Lance

The lance, like the javelin and the club were weapons that were not just essential in warfare but were also symbolic, representing strength and power. In Celtic mythology it was one of the four objects taken by the gods from one of the islands north of the world. The supreme god Lug possessed a lance, which was invincible and symbolic of fire. His lance or spear was also synonymous with the cauldron of Dagda, which was filled with blood that could destroy all around it, unless the lance was plunged within. The lance and the javelin in heraldry represent devotion to honour.

Lion / Leopard

The majestic lion represented strength, justice and courage attributed to military force, and in heraldry its depiction, depending on the stance, signified particular meanings. In the Middle Ages with the evolution of chivalry, the lion appeared more frequently and with greater importance, symbolizing royal power and fearless guardianship. The leopard was also emblematic but was essentially a replacement of the lion, as was the bear, symbolizing bravery and courageous deeds associated with war. In French heraldry, Napoleon was reputed to refer to the British soldiers as leopards.

The significance of the lion, like the swastika, has evolved and spread from other cultures, appearing as a symbol in early Celtic mythology. It also possessed certain magical attributes, and was believed to be able to resurrect the dead by its breath. It has always been regarded as the lord of the animals and king of the jungle. The lion of Saint Marc appeared in the illuminations of the famous Book of Durrow and has been depicted in varying forms, including engravings on objects, such as the Gundestrup cauldron, and in sculpted form on a Roman T-shaped aquamanile, housed at the Metropolitan Museum.

 **istletoe**

Today the mistletoe is associated with good fortune and fate, symbolic of winter and the festive season, and in Celtic tradition it also held a similar significance. This sacred plant gathered by the use of a sickle, was greatly utilized by the Druids due to its varying attributes, such as its curative powers, and was therefore used as a base in medicines and magical potions, which were believed to restore and invigorate the spirit. Aside from being able to cure all ills and evils, it was also regarded as an antidote to all poisons, but could equally be given as a poison when used in ritual ceremonies, such as sacrifices. The gathering of mistletoe in a ritual context was also symbolic, and picked on the sixth day of the moon it was considered especially potent and associated with fertility and royal succession.

Due to the importance of the oak in Celtic society, mistletoe found growing on it was believed to be the most sacred; however it was quite rarely found on this type of tree, as although a parasitic plant, it had difficulty in flourishing on the oak and so was generally picked from other sources.

Numbers

In Celtic tradition, certain numbers were considered important but more for their symbolic value, and each held their own signification. As well as recurring in mythology, they formed an essential part in the foundation of construction in cultures in general. They were also the basis for their spiritual and cosmic harmony, ensuring that there was an equilibrium and order within their existence.

Number One was symbolic of the world itself, the very beginning of all existence, the origin of the source of life, and was therefore a number central to spiritual being. The egg was also attributed to the number one and was symbolic of life and fertility; it also incorporated the cosmos and could be associated with the serpent, which in this context secretes an egg symbolic of ceaseless creativity. The serpent also represented renewal as well as heaven, earth and water.

Number Two was associated with the moon and lunar worship and the Celtic calendar was based on the moon, the Celts counting nights as opposed to days. It could also represent divinities or mythological characters associated in pairs such as Dagda and Ogma or the Druid and the boar, the boar and fertility, good and evil, night and day. Also certain divinities were depicted with the janiform head (double head).

Number Three was synonymous with the trinity, triads and triangle symbolism and when multiplied by itself gave the number nine, and was essentially considered the most significant of symbolic numbers in Celtic society. The mother-goddess could appear in triple form, as did many other aspects of their spiritual beliefs. In Celtic tradition, it was believed that triple representations possessed greater strength and potency and in mythology there are many references to three types of animal or days, secrets or three witches, as well as divinities such as Morrigann who could appear in triple form with her three magical birds. Three was also attributed to the sun.

Number Four was also important in mythology as objects or places could be depicted in fours. The sword belonging to Nuada, the Irish god-king of Tuatha De Dannan or the lance of Lug, were two of the four divine talismans brought from the four islands in the north. The four corners of the world and the four directions were symbolic. The lozenge attributed to fertility has four sides and could be depicted divided into four equal parts. Four was also attributed to the sun, in association with the swastika and the cross, both depicted with four parts and symbolic in solar worship.

Number Five was symbolic of the five Irish provinces, known also as the five kingdoms, the fifth province being the central one and surrounded by the other four. The five-pointed star, also known as the pentacle, is symbolic of life and health as well as immortality. Five also represented the unification of numbers two and three, both attributed to solar and lunar worship.

Number Six was linked to the beginning of life and the sun and the hexagram, a six-pointed star, is linked to Druidism.

Number Seven was often the fundamental equation used in construction amongst many cultures. The gold model boat of Broighter, County Derry, Ireland possesses seven oars, which in Celtic tradition symbolized the seven orifices of the body. In mythology, Culchulainn was depicted with seven fingers, seven toes, and seven pupils in each eye, with each pupil containing seven precious stones. The goddess Rhiannon, in Welsh legend, possesses magical birds, which bring joy or forgetfulness that can last for seven years. The image of the druidic cross portrays seven swords and seven is also the unification of numbers three and four.

Number Nine is the multiple of three, representing all aspects of the trinity in triple context as in the three cyclical changes, the three spheres and the three elements. When multiplied by itself it gives twenty-seven, which also recurs in mythology. Cuchulainn, whilst in conflict with a satirist, kills nine men in succession with his javelin, as well as massacreing Calatin and his twenty-seven sons in the epic of Cualnge. Morgane is also depicted in mythology, living on the island of Avalon with her nine sisters, although in certain traditions they have sometimes been represented as seven. Nine is also symbolic of a woman's period of gestation.

ak Tree

This highly revered tree renowned for its longevity and durability is the one most notably associated with ancient druidism, and in Celtic society, as well as in certain other cultures, it was also one of the most significant. They believed that it possessed curative and divine powers, symbolizing strength, solidity and sanctuary, and as the druids were also accorded the status of judge, with power over all, the oak therefore came to represent justice. It was a holy tree, symbolic in ritual worship and ceremonies. Its fruit, the acorn, was also important as it was attributed to fertility and immortality, and used by the Druids who believed it would enhance their power to divine. It was also the food of the pig, an animal also symbolic in Celtic tradition, including its association with the Otherworld along with the boar, which was emblematic to druidism and magic. In heraldry the oak tree also represents virtue, resilience and endurance.

Owl

Most notably symbolic for its wisdom, the owl also represented patience and was seen as a protector. Regarded as a significant mythological symbol throughout ancient history, the owl also possessed a dark side. It was a hunter tracking its prey with silence and rapidity, and associated with the night, which was when the day began in Celtic tradition, this bird of the forest with its ability to see in the dark, could also guide those to and from the Otherworld. Its wisdom could be called upon to reveal those who had deceived, and likewise the guilty could be transformed into an owl as punishment.

In later mythology, like the crow, the owl was also associated with magic and witchcraft. Eventually becoming emblematic, it has appeared in many forms and has remained an important bird in Welsh literature.

Patterns

The many elaborate and vivid designs and motifs distinctive of Celtic art derived from simple lines and curves which have adorned constructions, walls, stones and other objects since man was able to express himself. These recurring and widespread abstract shapes often represented a symbolic meaning, although they were possibly more ambiguous than the distinctive motifs of the spiral, swastika, triskele and cross.

The lozenge has been attributed to fertility and the feminine characteristics related to fertility, its shape has been compared to that of the vulva and the depiction of Sheela-na-gigs, who represented fertility, as well as creation and destruction, is undoubtedly a classic example of this supposition. It is also thought to represent the womb of Mother Earth and the reproduction of life, encapsulating the essence of planting and growing, but equally it could also represent the entrance to the Otherworld and its dark mysteries.

Motifs commonly found within the lozenge were **key patterns,** often divided into four equal parts and they could be synonymous with the **labyrinth** design, as the key shape could lead into the labyrinth. This design was not dissimilar to that of the **maze**, a more complex symbol, which proposes alternate paths to its sacred centre as opposed to the single path of the labyrinth. They represented a sacred place, symbolic of transformation, offering a spiritual journey, and the symbolism of the labyrinth notably in its classical form, continued into Christianity where it was usually incorporated into the pavements of places of worship. The **interlacing** patterns so frequently found, most probably originated from spiral shapes and were symbolic of the continuation of life without end. These motifs used by many different cultures, continued to flourish right through to Christianity, where later they could be found in the illuminated manuscripts of the monasteries, and they are still popular emblems for many Celtic organizations today.

Ram

The ram was one of the horned symbols, which represented vitality, decisive force and aggression: attributes that have often associated it with warriors and war divinities. Its symbolism had a shared significance with different ancient cultures, and in Egypt it was regarded as a temple creature, like the bull, and attributed to certain gods who were notably depicted with ram's heads or horns, such as Osiris. In Celtic symbolism, it was Cernunnos who sometimes appeared with the ram in its hybrid form, with a serpent's body, representing renewal and the cycle of life. The ram was symbolic of fertility and the procreative forces and was often used as a sacrificial offering, linking it with fire. It could also be associated with abundance, and the Romans attributed the ram to their god Bacchus.

The ram's image, and notably its head was incorporated into or appeared on various forms of jewellery, often on torques or bracelets, as well as being depicted on ancient coinage and was particularly significant in Gaul. The ram's head later became symbolic in Morris dancing, representing the mythical association between man and beast and the real world and that of the spiritual kind.

Salmon

The embodiment of wisdom and knowledge, this primeval symbol was held in high regard in Celtic tradition, and in Celtic mythology those who ate of this fish, were reputed to possess the 'knowledge' or 'wisdom of the salmon'. It also represented the sanctity of science and was considered all-knowing; and linked to the sacred fountain, it was the salmon that ate the nine hazelnuts of wisdom, which fell from the tree of knowledge. It was the ancient source of all things, representing the sanctity of water with its power to create or destroy. The Irish epic recounting the story of Finn portrays him as the first man to have eaten the 'Salmon of Knowledge'.

In 'Culhwch ac Olwen', taken from the Mabinogion, Arthur sends an embassy in search of the oldest animal in the kingdom that can reveal the whereabouts of Mabon, son of Modron, who was taken when he was three nights old. Finally they are led to the salmon of 'Llyn-Llyw', which tells them where Mabon is imprisoned.

The salmon was also regarded as prophetic and was symbolic to the Druids, who associated it with the final stages of transformation, transporting the souls, instinctively passing through rivers and seas until reaching its final spawning grounds. A fine example of fish transporting a person on its back is represented on the Gundestrup Cauldron.

Snake, Serpent

A complex symbol, the snake has appeared in many different forms throughout ancient mythology, appearing sometimes in various animal configurations such as with antlers, horns or as a multi ram-headed serpent. Cernunnos, lord of the animals was also sometimes identified with the snake appearing in this context, by certain Celtic tribes.

Symbolic of earth's mysteries, the snake was believed to possess healing powers and wisdom, knowledgeable of earth's secrets and strengths, and acting as companion to the Gods of these divine forces, as well as protecting the entrance to the otherworld. To the Celts snakes also represented the cycle of life, with their hibernation and their re-emergence in spring, the shedding of their skin, coupled with their phallic form, they were the embodiment of fertility and rebirth.

Snakes were also associated with the healing properties of water due to their fluid movement and form, linking them with rivers and the sea and also heaven and earth. Their venom had the power to take or give life and it is still used today in modern medicine.

Spirals

This simple yet potent motif has adorned many megalithic stones and monuments, particularly in Ireland, where at the burial site of New Grange, these forms can be found in the tumulus. It suggested the motion and fluidity of water and waves, as well as the turbulent forces of nature with its changing cycles, possessing within its abstract lines, the energy and movement of the elements. This primitive symbol was greatly utilized in Celtic tradition and its winding form echoed that of the serpent, signifying renewal, death and rebirth. It was widely used and recognised in ancient civilization and throughout the Bronze Age, influencing the essence and evolution of Celtic art forms and design. There are variations of its symbolism and it has also been represented as a double spiral, which was sometimes associated with the breasts of the mother-goddess or the triple spiral, which was similar to the triskele. The form of an S was also significant to the Celts, which they associated with the solar and sky divinities and which evoked a similarity to the spiral motif.

Stag / Deer

The stag represented not only dignity and strength but also symbolized fertility and the cyclical changes of nature, with the shedding of its antlers in spring and autumn and their eventual renewal. The antlers also represented the form of branches, affiliating it with the trees in the forest. Cernunnos, lord of the stags, but predominantly lord of all animals, has been portrayed with antlers, as depicted on the Gundestrup Cauldron. Finn, also known as the horned God and master of the animals of the forest, was able when turning his magic hood, to assume the appearance of any animal, including the stag.

Considered one of the most ancient of zoomorphic symbols, the stag and the deer, have often appeared in Celtic mythology. The white stag recognised for its grace, gentleness and docility was sometimes represented as a messenger to the otherworld and has been much referred to in legends. Flidais, who reigned over the forest fauna, travels her domain in a chariot drawn by stags.

They were also a prime source of food, and much prized by the hunter and have therefore also been associated with hunters and huntresses as well as saints, such as Saint David and Saint Patrick.

Stones

Stones were an important natural element in Celtic society and were used in the building of forts, for weaponry and served also as landmarks. Tombs, fonts and altars all represent an importance in a sacred context, and burial sites and places of ritual worship were distinctive by their stone formations. Certain ancient Celtic tribes believed that like the tree, stones also possessed an energy and force, housing the spirits of the deities. They also believed that stones with a hole in possessed a curative power and that by passing through the hole, you would be healed. These stones were also symbolic of the passage of life – inception, death and rebirth, and were commonly situated at burial sites. According to Irish legend, the stone of Fal represented a link to earth and destiny, and was symbolic of sovereignty in connection with Ireland.

The symbolisms of stone varied, and they have been attributed to fertility, the form of many menhirs perhaps implying a phallic significance.

Stones were however also a primeval source of communication; throughout ancient history they have been used as a statement, such as the ancient Egyptian pyramids, as well as for transmitting messages and information and also scriptures. The sacred writing of ogham, attributed to Scotland, Wales and

Ireland, was notched on stone and wood. Creative expression was demonstrated through sculpting, carving and engraving, and included many symbols dating from the early Neolithic period onwards, including the remarkable Pictish stone carvings, depicting many simple forms of iconography.

Able to withstand the forces of nature, many examples of sacred stone sites, including cairns, such as the one at Newhaven are still in evidence today as are many of the ancient menhirs.

The ancient 'Stone of Fal', believed to possess mystical properties, can be found on the royal and sacred hill of Tara, County Meath, Ireland.

Stone Circle

Swan

Representing purity and love, with its white plumage, the ancient Celts considered the swan as a sacred and solar animal. Its gracefulness, gave it an affinity with women and in Celtic mythology, lady-swans on descending to earth from the Otherworld, would free themselves from their feathers and appear naked, usually near water. The Irish hero Cuchulainn was able to follow in flight bird-women from the Otherworld that had taken the form of swans. Often appearing in pairs, messengers of the divinities from the Otherworld would take the form of a swan, as did the gods of love, such as Fand, Libane and Derbforgaill. The god Oenghus transforms himself into a swan to rejoin his loved one Caer, who changes into the same bird every alternate year.

It was and still is considered taboo to eat the meat of a swan or to hunt it, and in heraldry they are royal animals, often depicted in pairs. Swans and other water birds such as ducks and geese have appeared in varying forms of Celtic art, sharing a similar importance.

Swastika / Svastika

This ancient symbol has appeared throughout various cultures for thousands of years and it is believed that its simple design and significance held a widespread appeal, which resulted in its appropriation by many countries. The svastika, a word originally deriving from the Sanskrit, symbolized 'luck' and 'well-being', and in Indo-European cultures it notably appeared made as a mark on a person or object in this symbolic form.

In Celtic civilization with its connection to the sun, this motif was particularly popular and could also be associated with the solar-wheel; and like the circle and the cross, it possessed certain mysticism, and was equally considered one of the symbols of life.

The swastika has appeared on many early art forms and was particularly present on objects found originating from the Greeks and Hittites, as well as the Celts. Some of these objects include pottery, cups and shields, as well as stone carvings, such as the example found at County Kerry, Ireland, believed to be of pagan origin. A stunning example of jewellery includes an ancient Iranian necklace found at Kaluraz, currently on

display at the National Museum of Iran. The swastika was also incorporated into religious architecture, such as churches and temples, and there are some similarities between this symbol and certain forms of the cross, such as the cross of Saint Brigitte.

Sword

In Celtic mythology the sword possessed a divine power, and was attributed to Nuada, the Irish god-king of the Tuatha De Dannan, who later became known as the king with the silver hand or arm. His sword was one of four magical objects and was infallible, killing all those that it touched. Important swords, more significantly the long sword, were also attributed to heroes as well as gods, and often the most highly decorated of these weapons could depict their own tales of victory and heroic battle. The long sword was also attributed to the light and solar forces, possessing a royal power symbolic of war. Blacksmiths were also regarded as superior because of their ability to produce such fine weaponry from sacred elements such as fire and water, and with the expansion of the Celts, their craftsmanship developed, as did the sword.

In Arthurian legend, Arthur becomes king by removing the sword from a stone, which he named Caledvwlch, which however is perhaps most renowned as his sword Excalibur.

Torque

The symbolic importance of the torque is quite ambiguous; it was reputed to harness special powers, and on the Gundestrup cauldron Cernonnus appears with one in his hand, whilst wearing another around his neck. Other Celtic deities have been depicted wearing a torque, and in Irish mythology, the judge and poet Morann wore a necklace, which could enlarge or retract itself depending on his good or bad judgement. The account of the torque belonging to Saint Cynog, also makes reference to the keeping of a promise, and so it also came to symbolize the value of truth; therefore, promises made before the torque were not to be broken.

Usually consisting of many intertwined strands, either in fine metal, bronze or sometimes gold, the half crescent shape of the torque was also thought to have been symbolic of the moon. Many sacred sites of ritual worship relating to the sun and the moon were of similar form or circular, and the circle with its magical and cosmic connotations was especially important in Celtic tradition. The torque was a distinguished piece of jewellery and the highly decorated pieces symbolized status and nobility. In battle, Celtic warriors have been portrayed fighting naked and wearing a torque.

Tree

The tree was undoubtedly the most ancient and omnipotent of plant symbolism, as it represented the link between the sky and the earth, with its branches reaching upwards towards the heavens and its roots spreading downwards towards the underworld. It was considered the embodiment of the universe itself, with its continual renewal of life through the changing seasons. As Celtic art evolved, the tree of life first depicted in simple form, gradually changed into a more elaborate image with intertwining branches and leaves. The tree was also attributed to the gods and was often the object of worship. The Celts believed that it housed the spirits of certain deities, as well as possessing spiritual energies and strength, and it was regarded a punishable crime to damage a tree.

In Celtic tradition, trees were also associated with knowledge, bearing the fruits of science and wisdom and were of particular significance to the druids. They believed that wood from certain types of tree possessed special holy and magical qualities: trees such as the oak, ash, yew and hazel. The simple writing method of Ogham, considered sacred and magical, was used to carve or notch on stone and wood and each letter represented the name of a tree, and it was therefore also referred to as the tree-alphabet. Woods and forests were magical and mysterious, sheltering different animals, many of which were symbolic or sacred to the Celts. These places were also associated with the Druids who performed ritual ceremonies in certain open woodland spaces known as groves, and these holy areas could offer sanctuary as well as a place to teach and for clans to gather. Some clans took their names from certain trees and individuals could also be named after a tree, and would be identified as daughter or son of Rowan or Hazel for example.

The trees, which shared a particular importance in Celtic tradition, included the oak, apple, yew, hazel, ash, birch, beech, rowan, pine, poplar, olive, walnut, cypress and the linden.

Trinity / Triad / Triangle

In Celtic tradition these recurring motifs were synonymous with the number three which was one of the most significant numbers in their society, as it was in other Indo-European cultures. They represented the threefold nature of the fundamental elements of their spiritual being, which is evident as much of their symbolism appeared in threes. Their Mother Goddess was depicted with triple connotations as are the cyclical changes of life, which are also represented as three – life, death and rebirth, accompanied by the three spheres – earth, sea and sky, and the three elements of the earth – water, air and fire, also – past, present and future. Characters and creatures in mythology were sometimes depicted with three heads or were represented in the context of three, such as the triad consisting of Teutates, Taranis and Esus who shared a particular importance to the Gauls.

The spiritual concept of the trinity continued into Christianity but attributed to God, with the Father, Son and Holy Ghost. Like the triskele, motifs symbolizing the unity of three have appeared universally in varying forms; such as the triangle, represented in simple decorative art form, and the triquetra, meaning 'three cornered' in Latin, a more complex design, which has been found carved on stones. In Ireland it is believed that the shamrock originally derived from this symbol and was first adopted by Saint Patrick, who following the introduction of Christianity used this pagan sign to illustrate the Holy Trinity.

Triskele / Triskelion

In ancient history these symbols have appeared in similar forms, their names deriving from the Greek meaning 'three-legged'. Influenced by the Greeks, variations of these abstract symbols, associated with many European Celtic tribes, developed and, like the swastika, its symbolism and simple characteristics became largely dispersed. Early representations of this symbol appeared on the ancient coins of the Syracusans from around 300 BC. The three circles of the triskelion were reputed to call upon three fates, possessing magical attributes, but also like the triskele, it represented the seasons and the three cycles of life in the material world, life, death and rebirth. With its powerful connotations relating to the number three, the triskele also symbolized the three spheres – earth, sea and sky, in addition to the three important earth elements – water, air and fire. They suggested movement, with no beginning and no end, evocative of neolithical spiral forms, and like the circle and the wheel, they had solar and cosmic origins. Their symbolism has been depicted on various objects, weaponry and jewellery, as well as appearing notably on Pictish stone carvings, followed later by their introduction into Christian manuscripts.

In Celtic tradition they represented the Threefold Sister Goddess and the Wiccan Threefold Mother Goddess, symbolizing mother, maiden and crone.

Water

From the beginning of time, water, like fire and air has remained an integral and essential element of the earth. The infinity of the sea held deep mysteries, and associated with the mother goddess, it was the primitive source of all things. Springs and fountains became synonymous with healing, purification and renewal, and deities, notably attributed to the sun such as Sulis or the mother goddess Brigid, became associated with healing waters, their image often found close by. Later with the introduction of Christianity numerous saints were also linked to these sacred places. But it was eventually the Romans who developed the custom of bathing in them, founding places such as Bath in England, although its original source was discovered by a wandering leper with his infected herd of swine, which were miraculously healed after bathing in the water.

In Celtic legend, the cauldron was symbolic of healing and rejuvenation as well as being sacrificial. In lakes, rivers and even marshland ritual sacrifices were made; the druids carried out sacrificial ceremonies to the deities, in which votive offerings were made of either objects of personal value or in living form, and human remains and other items have been discovered by archaeologists in these watery graves, preserved in the marshes.

Water was also associated with fertility, and in the story of Conchobar's Conception, it is Nesa who becomes pregnant after drinking water containing two worms. Today, the healing and purifying powers of water are still important, with the use of holy water in baptism and with our need to benefit from its curative properties in thermal baths and springs.

*The Hot Springs of Bath were dedicated
to the Celtic Goddess Sulis*

Wheel

The wheel is a complex symbol and to the druids it represented an important connection with the worship of the sun and the solar and celestial deities. Attributed to the Celtic god Taranis, master of the sky, it was known also as the wheel of life or the cosmic wheel, possessing mystic connotations, symbolizing the seasons and the flow of night and day. In Roman mythology Jupiter was also associated with the wheel, and in Irish mythology the god Lug was sometimes known as 'the god at the wheel' as was the mystical Irish druid Mog Ruth, who was also referred to as 'the servant of the wheel'. In later Celtic tradition, the spoked wheel developed greater significance and wheel-shaped brooches were reputed to symbolize power and strength.

Wolf

The wolf like the dog was equally regarded with positive or negative connotations, which varied according to different cultures. It was the supreme hunter, possessing a greater intelligence and nobility than that of the dog, and sharing the same attributes as the lion and bear. In certain cultures, such as that of the Celts, the wolf was recognised for its wisdom, and could be a source of inspiration as well as guidance, which was why it was often attributed to the spirits of the otherworld. Its inner strength could overcome the darker forces of the underworld, possessing deep and mysterious powers. In Celtic tradition the druids believed that by placing the hide of an animal, such as the bull, the bear or the wolf over the body, it could induce divinatory dreams.

In many cultures, the wolf was notably symbolic of war and death, and therefore the warrior. The Romans associated the wolf in this context, and Odin the Norse god of war, was depicted as commanding a pair of wolves. Again like the dog, following the introduction of Christianity, the wolf became associated with evil forces and was even considered in some cultures as demonic. An animal generally symbolic of the night and the moon, it eventually often became portrayed as the companion of witches.

The wolf has been frequently depicted in mythology, appearing in various guises, and its image has appeared in different forms; such as on the carved Pictish stone of Ardoss, Scotland or the wolf's head sculpture found in Spain. Many examples of various canine statuettes were uncovered at the Roman temple of Nodins, Lydney, Gloucester. Built on an ancient Iron Age hill fort, the temple was believed to be symbolic of healing, and the findings also included a small bronze statue of a wolfhound.

Wren

The wren was the sacred bird of the old Celtic kingdom, the Isle of Man and of the druids, and was regarded by them as superior to all birds. It symbolized good fortune and wealth and the Celts believed that by killing a wren at the beginning of the new year, it would bring them luck. In Christianity, the ritual killing of a wren took place on Saint Stephen's day. The robin and the wren were regarded as birds of hope by sailors, who believed that the feather of a wren would protect them. In Wales and Scotland it is considered unlucky to kill them.

 # ew Tree

Possibly the most ancient and noble of all trees, the yew represented life and death in Celtic tradition. Its fruit could be used to heal, or equally like the mistletoe, used as a poison; and warriors used the toxic juice from its berries on their arrow tips. Other weapons were constructed out of its wood, such as lances, bows and shields as well as dagger handles. The lance of the supreme god Lug was reputed to be made of yew. With its dual characteristics, the yew was associated with the Otherworld, considered along with the oak and the apple as a tree of life, and because of its curative or mortal properties it played a significant part in Druidism. Its association with death also symbolized it as a funeral tree, presumably because of its connection with the souls of the dead, their passing into the otherworld and their resurrection; and it was often planted around or near cemeteries.

The sacred writing of Ogham was engraved on wood using special sticks fabricated from the yew as well as that of the hazel. In mythology its association with magic and wisdom continued with the salmon, which ate the berries from the yew of Mugna, after they fell into the water. The yew has been linked to the cypress, another sacred and evergreen tree, also recognised for its longevity, and like the oak, the yew, is known also for its durability, and it in fact possesses a longer life span. In heraldry it is symbolic of resurrection and faith.

CHAPTER THREE

THE EVOLUTION OF CELTIC SYMBOLISM

Many artists, writers, designers and architects have been greatly influenced by their Celtic heritage throughout the centuries; influences which have evolved and developed in different cultures over the passage of time. Rich with colour and imagination, these cultures have interpreted and adapted ancient art and symbology to their own iconography, encompassing mythology and legend, all of which have contributed to being a source of inspiration to those who have played an important part in shaping the future.

With the introduction of Christianity, symbolic styles were already beginning to develop, yet they were also still retaining much of the ancient and more traditional influences, which went on to inspire works such as the Book of Kells, the Book of Durrow and the Lindisfarne Gospels. Literature equally captured the essence of earlier folklore, producing epics such as those of Arthur and the Mabinogion. Heraldry itself was greatly inspired by Celtic motifs and zoomorphic imagery and the simple iconography produced by the Iron Age Picts by carving into stone, would later become a valuable source of inspiration in Scottish heraldry.

In the early part of the Middle Ages many new Romanesque, Gothic style churches and cathedrals were being constructed, often incorporating designs and motifs influenced by Greek,

Roman and Celtic antiquity. One popular motif often incorporated into the grand pavement designs of several of these buildings was the labyrinth, examples of which can still be admired in the great cathedrals of Chartres and Amiens, in France; another example is that of the Duomo, in Sienna, Italy. These complex symbols became especially popular around the twelfth century in Christianity and were usually associated with pilgrimage. Walking the labyrinth represented undertaking a spiritual pilgrimage as opposed to perhaps making the actual journey to Jerusalem. However many of these labyrinths were later destroyed or removed. Those of Chartres and Amiens are particularly outstanding examples, with that of Amiens possessing other bold geometric designs, such as the swastika motif and varying key or maze style patterns. Its symbolic meaning has meant that from early civilizations right through to the twentieth century, it has continued to hold a spiritual importance in many different cultures, with new representations that have been created in certain public areas.

In the nineteenth and early part of the twentieth century, Roman style churches, chapels and other religious monuments were also being built, inspired by the same influences; and façades and interiors frequently included spiral forms and elaborate interlacing motifs. Celtic themes could often adorn walls, floors and ceilings, as well as being incorporated in engravings, masonry and other religious objects. Ireland in particular, was especially enamoured by these ancient art forms and symbolism.

The influences of Celtic art and mythology also inspired other innovative creations on a larger scale, such as the building of a town. Born in 1704, John Wood was an architect, driven by a vision to create and enlarge much of the town of Bath. At the age of seventeen this young architect was already involved in property speculation, but also had designs of a grander and more significant scale, which were to build a great town. However, following the withdrawal of his original sponsor, Wood returned to London, spending a considerable time in the capital before returning to Bath. Having secured new financial backing, he found himself finally in a position to realize his most ambitious project yet. By his early twenties, he had begun to establish himself as Bath's most significant architect, creating buildings of neoclassical design, yet combined with the essence of ancient mythology and legend, shrouding the town with a certain air of mysticism. Later research speculated that during his stay in London, the young architect had in fact become a freemason, indications of which became later apparent in the masonry, the mouldings and architraves of the exteriors and interiors of his buildings, which revealed carvings and symbolic icons associated with the practice of freemasonry.

Inspired by the legend of King Bladud, John Wood found the very soul and foundations of his vision from the ancient sites of Stonehenge and Stanton Drew. Echoing the geometric precision with which each stone had been placed and the distance calculated between their placement and its symbolic importance, were the factors which played a critical part in the placement and the alignment of the buildings that would form the new Bath. His great vision was continued and eventually completed by his son, John Wood (junior), following his death in 1754.

Although ancient art and mythology had already to a certain degree contributed towards influencing the approach to architecture, art and design, its more traditional concept really began to undergo dramatic changes towards the end of the 19th century with the beginning of the Art Nouveau movement. Following in the path of the arts and crafts period initiated by designers such as William Morris in 1861 and disaffected by the conforms of Victorian design, the Art Nouveau movement introduced a new and lucid form of expression. These designers combined geometric shapes with fluid and sinuous lines, flowing and twisting, incorporating many of nature's elements sometimes accompanied with graceful feminine figures. These were greatly influenced by earlier forms of art, deriving from the Gothic and Rococo periods but also combining some of the subtlety and simplicity of Japanese art. Norse and Celtic art was also a key element in influencing much of the art and design during this period, particularly the latter, which is apparent in many examples of artwork produced by the renowned artists of its time.

Archibald Knox was one such artist whose work was greatly inspired by the Celtic manuscripts as well as Celtic and Norse art forms found on his native home, the Isle of Man. Having studied at the Douglas School of Art, he left the Island in 1897 to teach in London and at the height of the Art Nouveau period, he began designing for the London firm of Liberty & Co. There he produced finely crafted metalware, including the more memorable 'Cymric' silverware collection, followed later by the 'Tudric' pewter series. These works included finely detailed interlacing symbols, vegetal forms with fluid lines and curves, which became synonymous with the Art Nouveau movement, and eventually established him as one of the leading artists and designers of this era.

Archibald Knox went on to design many notable and innovative pieces including jewellery, vases, clocks and textiles as well as producing illustrative work and memorial stonework, inspired by the early Celtic and Norse crosses. He eventually returned to the Isle of Man, where he continued to teach art, later becoming a renowned water-colour artist.

During the late 19th century, the period known as Celtic Revival had in itself evolved into a significantly recognisable movement and continued to flourish. Like Archibald Knox, many of the great symbolist painters were inspired by Celtic and Norse mythology accompanied by other European influences, such as some of the early renaissance art produced in Italy. Even Da Vinci's imagination did not escape the intricate interlacing and fluid, weaving interwoven lines of these ancient cultures.

In Scotland in the 1890's, artist John Duncan was in the process of establishing himself as one of the leading representatives of this new movement. Born in Dundee in 1866, he studied art at Dundee High School and later went on to teach abroad, spending time in America, Antwerp and Italy. The latter played an important role in influencing his later works, as well as Byzantine art, which was also a rich source of inspiration to many of the prominent artists during this period. In 1880, he began his career as an illustrator spending part of his time in London before heading to the continent and then finally returning home to Dundee where he eventually met Patrick Geddes in 1891, who was to become a key figure in influencing his future projects. John Duncan's growing interest in Celtic mythology, music, literature and Gaelic, inspired him to produce what were considered some of his most notable works. Projects such as 'The Evergreen', a publication which involved the collaboration of his new mentor Patrick Geddes, produced poems such as 'Anima Celtica' which appeared in an 1895 issue and included an elaborate illustration representing an inspired Celtic theme. The celebrated murals in Ramsey Gardens, three of which incorporated borders of Celtic knotwork were equally influenced by Celtic legends as were many of his commissions, which included adapting famous works such as the book of Kells. In 1903, on returning home to Scotland after teaching fine art in Chicago, Duncan eventually settled in Edinburgh where he continued to produce many of his most memorable works. Celtic revival continued to flourish, combined with the Art Nouveau movement, spreading into Europe and reaching its peak at the beginning of the first world war.

In Ireland, The Celtic Revival or renaissance movement as it was also known, was equally evolving and establishing itself as an important period of artistic expression, combined with deep national feeling. The years of political subjugation and unrest were finally surfacing, utilizing the creative arts as a medium, and began to materialize with greater significance towards the end of Ireland's Great Famine. Drawing inspiration from Celtic mythology, artists, writers, musicians, designers and architects were at once able to identify themselves and their growing need for independence with the heroes and spiritual symbolism of their Celtic heritage. Many of their forebears, having already fled to Ireland during the Roman invasion and the conflicts created by the Angles and Jutes, had already suffered centuries of repression at the hands of these invaders. From around 1840, the direction of Irish art began changing and the rapidly growing young Irish movement found its voice through a new artistic media, especially in the 1870's when the various campaigns were gaining strength. Many of the significant artists of this period, expressed the essence of their Celtic past, encompassing folklore and mythology, in poetry, paintings, books and plays and by the 1880's the literary scene was positively incandescent within this Irish cultural revival. Exhibitions were being held, not just in Ireland but in Europe, and numerous institutions and organizations were also being formed, such as the Gallery of Modern Art, founded by Hugh Lane, and the Abbey Theatre established in the early 1900's, associated with Lady Gregory and several of Ireland's leading playwrights and poets, including William Butler Yeats. His brother Jack, also a notable figure and renowned painter during this era, was among many of the artists to be influenced by his country's history.

Monuments also became important and often represented a symbolic association, such as the bronze statue of Cù Chulainn by sculptor Oliver Sheppard, which was put up in remembrance of the Easter Rebellion of 1916. The bronze, entitled 'The Death of Cù Chulainn' is housed in the General Post Office at Dublin, which had formerly been the headquarters of the Irish volunteers and the provisional government and included members such as the renowned poet, Patrick Pearse, who after joining the Gaelic League eventually became the editor of its weekly newspaper also referred to as the 'Sword of Light'.

In contemporary Irish artwork murals such as those depicted by the Republican and Loyalist movements frequently incorporate Celtic images, which have continued to play a symbolic role in expressing their political message. Cù Chulainn, the Celtic cross and the sunburst are a few of the recurring symbols that have been represented.

The Celtic Revival movement continued to develop in parallel with that of Art Nouveau, and much of the new religious architecture and ornamentation in Ireland included many familiar Celtic symbols and designs, such as the intricate interlacing, spirals and labyrinth motifs, inspired by the illuminated manuscripts of the early Irish monasteries, and works such as the Book of Kells. These early works would later provide a source of inspiration for many of the embroidered motifs on traditional Gaelic costumes, and their comparison with the engraved motifs on ancient Celtic armories, such as helmets, swords and shields, reveal a distinctive similarity. Book covers, jewellery and engravings were amongst a number of the decorative works produced by literary figures and artists, also epitomizing the influences of their historic past.

In Brittany, the desire to identify with their Celtic heritage was equally important to its peoples. As in Ireland, the Bretons incorporated many different aspects of Celtic design into their art, which was perhaps especially apparent earlier on, in their traditional embroidered costumes. However by the early 1920's, the traditional elements of their art began to merge with more contemporary design and in 1923, three Breton artists founded a movement referred to as the 'Seiz Breur Movement' which was to change the concept of Breton art and which would continue to flourish until 1944. Inspired to combine modern art with traditional styles, Jeanne Malivel, René-Yves Creston and James Bouillé created 'Ar Seiz Breur' meaning 'seven brothers' in Breton, a name chosen for its symbolic meaning implying unity. The idea was borne following a meeting in a restaurant at Folgöet, where Jeanne Malivel proposed to the group of friends present, who included the Crestons, the Marquers, the Régimers and Yan Caroff, to combine their talents and form an amicable association of artists.

Motif - Joseph Savina Seiz Breur Movement

This innovative movement eventually involved the work and close collaboration of many different artists, and as in Ireland, it also changed the future of their literature, music, fashion and design. They were greatly influenced by Celtic mythology and art, and incorporated many varying forms of Celtic motifs, such as spirals, circles and interlacing patterns into furniture, ceramic and textile design. Jeanne Malivel and James Bouillé both produced several elaborate pieces of embroidered work, with distinctive Celtic motifs ; whilst other artists such as Yves Hémar, Joseph Savina and Jacques Philippe produced furniture during the mid 1920's and 30's which included beautifully crafted inlays featuring Celtic based designs. The 'throne' designed by Jacques Philippe in 1929, is an outstanding example. This revival resulted in the creation of various organizations, including the Celtic Institute formed in 1942. The 'Seiz Breur' union eventually collapsed in 1944 following political tensions involving the war and the need for Brittany to be recognised as an independent country by certain minority movements. The 'Seiz Breur Movement' is still regarded as an integral part of the Breton Culture and the country's Celtic influences continue to inspire many of its artists today.

The following symbols described in the final section of this book, reflect their evolution from their original representation in ancient history, to their iconography in the present day. Over the centuries, these few symbols are ones that have consistently re-occurred, and their images have undoubtedly altered; however it is interesting to note that their basic symbolism and popularity have remained relatively unchanged.

THE EVOLUTION OF CELTIC SYMBOLS

Evolution of the Cockerel

Due to its symbolic relevance, it is no surprise that the cockerel should have been adopted as an emblem. It is notably associated with the French who during the Middle Ages engraved their coinage with its image and it was later adopted in 1789 by the French revolutionary leaders. Despite Napoleon's decision to replace the image of the cockerel with that of the eagle, convinced that the latter would be more representative of France's invincible empire, it was reintroduced again in the nineteenth century when it appeared on the flags and buttons of the National Guard, and during the First World War, it represented courage and readiness to fight. Its image also appeared on the twenty franc gold coin, the great seal, and again on the gates of the Presidential residence, the Elysée Palace. It can also notably be found on some French postage stamps.

Today the image of the French cockerel is associated with their national rugby team, and it again enjoyed new fame as the country's emblem during World Cup football.

Evolution of the Cross

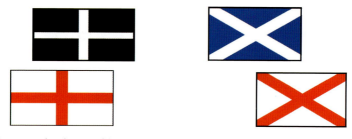

With the evolution of heraldry, variations of the cross became incorporated into shields, banners and flags, and Kings and countries eventually became recognizable by their blazon or crest. Flags with crosses were notable during the crusades, with the different colour of each cross generally representing its country of origin.

A few of these examples include the **Saint George's cross**, representative of Saint George, patron saint of England and its national flag, whose design has formed the basis for other flags common to Northern Ireland.

The Saintt Andrew's Cross, or the National Flag of Alba, is composed of a white saltire on a blue background, dating back to the eighth century and is associated with the legend of King Angus, who led the Picts in battle against the Saxon chief, Athelstane. With his army surrounded by the enemy, Angus prayed for a miracle, which appeared the following day in the form of a white cross in the blue sky, and drawing courage from this sign, Angus went on to defeat Athelstane. The saltire represents the cross on which Saint Andrew was crucified, therefore becoming emblematic to the Scots and was later worn by the guardians of Scotland.

The Cornish flag known as **Saint Piran's flag** (or Saint Michael's) is a white cross on a black background and the actual origin of its design still remains uncertain. The legend surrounding its design is based on Saint Piran, who came to Cornwall from Ireland in the fifth century to convert its people to Christianity. Cornwall was renowned for its tin mining, and Saint Piran eventually became the patron saint of tin-miners. Whilst he was smelting tin one day, he was surprised when the white-hot fluid, which had poured onto the black ashes beneath where he was working, formed the shape of a cross.

When Cornwall came under Saxon influence, many of the then Celtic settlers fled to Brittany, whose flag at the time was a black cross on a white background, and is supposed to have influenced the Cornish design. In heraldry, the ancient Colville family arms in Scotland consists of a black cross on a white shield.

Saint Patrick's Cross is notably associated with the British regiments and is therefore not widely recognised by the Irish people, even during the celebrations for Saint Patrick's day.

Evolution of the Dove

For thousands of years, the dove has possessed many symbolic attributes and with it's gentle but fearless nature, was thought to be one of the first creatures to be domesticated by man. The dove's symbolism was significant in many of the ancient cultures and was frequently attributed to the deities, such as the goddess Aphrodite, whom in Greek mythology represented love, as well as Venus who was also symbolic of love and fertility. The dove was also the Romans' sacrificial bird to Venus and her chariot was supposedly drawn by white doves. It was also associated with Adonis and revered by Astarte, where its attributes possessed more erotic significations, and to the Assyrians it was the sacred bird of Semiramis who transformed herself into the form of a dove. Particularly to the Greeks and the Romans it was a bird which represented love and devotion, and its image appeared in early Roman art forms such as mosaics. The Romans were also reputedly breeders of the dove, using it as a messenger and constructing large dovecotes; but the dove was equally regarded as a messenger of the gods, and could also represent man's spirit or soul in pleasure or in death. Its image was sometimes depicted on Roman tombs and monuments, and with an olive branch in its beak it symbolized eternal peace for the departed soul.

With its widespread iconography, particularly after the introduction of Christianity, the dove's symbolism gradually developed, spreading into other cultures, becoming a popular image of hope, love and peace. In 1949, a dove painting by Picasso became nationally representative of peace on earth, when it appeared in a poster campaign by the 'World Peace Congress'. Since then, the image of the dove has been used by peace campaigners and organizations worldwide and is also sometimes associated with the white-ribbon, which has currently been symbolic for more than thirty years.

In 2003, at the seventy-fifth Annual Academy Film Awards in

Los Angeles, dove pins were worn by many of the attending celebrities, symbolizing the need for world peace. In China the dove is symbolic of longevity and peace and in Japan, depicted with a sword, it represented the end of war and the beginning of peace.

In certain areas of North America, the 'Mourning Dove' is considered a game bird and is therefore hunted; however the state of Wisconsin adopted the bird as its official symbol in 1971, prohibiting its destruction by residents. Dove hunting is still regarded as a game sport in other countries.

Evolution of the Dragon

Since the first invasion of Britain by the Romans, the red dragon has appeared on standards and devices throughout various battles, from the Battle of Hastings in 1066, to appearing as the emblem of Owain Glyndwr in 1404, in his retaliation against the English.

King Arthur's father was referred to as Uther Pendragon, 'chief of warriors', or 'head leader', as the Welsh word for 'Pen' meant head and 'dragon' meant 'leader', or the term 'Draig' was associated with the 'warrior'. He also used the dragon as his symbol.

The red dragon reappeared as the standard of Henry Tudor, during the battle of Bosworth in 1485. Supported by the Welsh, Henry defeated King Richard III. The green and white livery colours of the Tudor family presumably became synonymous with the red dragon symbol and eventually representative of the Welsh people.

The red dragon has also been represented on other armories, including its portrayal in the Bayeux tapestry.

Evolution of the Falcon and the Hawk

Both these birds, like the eagle, have appeared throughout mythology, representing gods and goddesses or kings, as well as being symbolic in ancient legends. In ancient Egypt, gods such as the sun god Ra, or Horus the lower god of Egypt were associated with these birds, and Horus could appear in the form of either one. The hawk, like the eagle was regarded as a solar bird. They were considered royal birds and Egyptian kings were often depicted as falcon-headed and soldiers have been represented carrying a falcon standard in battle.

There have been references to the falcon in Norse mythology, and in Celtic mythology the falcon and the hawk were regarded as more malevolent than the eagle, representing the hunter and the warrior and appeared as ornamentation on objects such as helmets and other armories.

The Falcon Stone, in Perthshire, Scotland dates from around 980 A.D. Legend has it that during the Battle of Luncarty, a local countryman and his two sons working in a nearby field, witnessing the failing courage of King Kenneth III's men against the Danes, went to the king's aid and helped him to conquer their attackers. In gratitude, the king ordered the release of one of his falcons, proclaiming that wherever it flew and landed, would belong to the countryman and his sons. The falcon finally alighted on a large standing stone and it is this stone, which is still referred to today as the Falcon's Stone. The countryman and his sons were believed to be the ancestors of the Hays family and the Hays family's coat of arms features a falcon and three blood-stained shields, supposedly representative of the father and his sons.

The Falcon is also associated with the Isle of Man, as it appears as one of the supporters of its shield on the island's coat of arms. In 1405, John Stanley was given the Isle of Man by Henry IV and in return he was to pay homage to him by giving him two falcons. It was agreed that he would continue this tradition with every other future king of England on their coronation day and this continued up until the coronation of George IV in 1822.

Today the Peregrine Falcon is symbolic of the National Wildlife Federation, due to the fact that it is at risk of becoming an endangered species.

Evolution of the Griffon

The Griffon has been depicted in various forms throughout ancient history, with each culture representing this creature with its own particular symbolism, although generally the griffon shared similar significations. It was a creature closely associated with the deities, particularly Apollo, Athena and Nemesis and was often depicted pulling the chariots of the gods, and in Asia Minor examples of the griffon symbol were found in Apollo's temple. They were symbolic of protection, depicted also on Egyptian tombs as well as appearing on palace walls as protector of the king and his treasures.

In early art work, their representations often differed: the Romans for example portrayed them with the beaks of an eagle, symbolizing might and justice, along with courage and intelligence, and they appeared in friezes in temples

such as those of Antoninus and Faustina. Early Celtic depictions were characteristically not dissimilar to those of the Romans. In Crete, they also appeared in frescoes and their wingless representations were generally less aggressive than those of the Greeks, the Romans and the Scythians, where its image was engraved on Scythian gold which was protected by these creatures, killing anyone who dared to rob them. Their image has been carved into table supports, examples of which were found in Rome and Pompeii and they were also represented on tapestries and featured on gold work.

Due to its varying iconography and the introduction of Christianity, it became difficult to establish whether the Griffon represented good or evil, and it was initially attributed to Satan. However perhaps due to its solar aspects and its association with the sky and therefore heaven, it was eventually perceived in a more divine light, symbolic of resurrection, and by the nineteenth century was generally considered harmless. In 1784, Thomas Pennant on a tour of Wales, made several illustrations of medieval tombstones in Bangor, including one depicting a lion and a griffon passant accompanied by a cross in a circle. The griffon represented divine power and the guardianship of the divine. Thomas Pennant declared that this symbolism was representative of the embracing of early Christianity of the nations of our Island. The griffon also appeared engraved on a silver Elizabethan chalice, known as the 'Derwent Chalice' made in 1584, which was passed down to the chapel of St Cyprian, built by the monks of Welbeck Abbey. The griffon was featured with other engravings, symbolic of the elements, such as the eagle, the phoenix, the turtle and the orange, representing earth: however the significance of the griffon on the chalice has remained a mystery.

In heraldry, the griffon represented wisdom and fortitude, as well as bravery and valour, and was notably portrayed with ears and a feathered neck usually in a rampant posture standing on one hind leg, with the other leg and claw raised and facing left. In clan heraldry the griffon could often appear with other devices, such as in its representation on the flag of the Irish 'O'Cahan' clan, where it appears with five other emblems; however its actual symbolism in this context remains undefined.

Representations of the griffon continued to appear throughout medieval history, and in 1698 it became the emblem of the town of Saint Brieuc, Brittany, towards the end of the ancient regime, replacing that of the eagle, which appeared on the town seal. The griffon was blazoned on their coat of arms and is still their official emblem today, being later modified in 1985. The English town of Budleigh Salterton in Devon, also features the griffon on its crest as part of their civic arms, combining those of Sir Walter Raleigh who was born in nearby Hayes Barton.

In 1876, the Philadelphia Museum of Art was founded, originally inspired by the Victoria & Albert Museum, London, and features bronze cast statues of the griffon, which are currently situated on the museum roof, representative of their nature as guardians of treasure. The Museum still currently uses the griffon as its logo. During World War II, one of the spitfires produced was referred to as the 'Griffon Spitfire' due to its powerful engine and its ability to fly at great speeds and heights. In 1953, a heraldic sculpture of a griffon was made in celebration of the Queen's Coronation as part of the 'Ten Queen's Beasts' and is now currently housed at Kew Gardens in London.

Throughout history there have been numerous written references to these mythical creatures and much hypothesis regarding their derivation. In ancient mythology, the Greeks and the Assyrians believed that the vulture was a descendant of the griffon and today one of these great birds, referred to as 'Ruppell's Griffon Vulture', can be found in countries such as Africa. Griffon vultures have also been sighted in Britain, for instance in 1843 in County Cork, Ireland, and again in England in 1927. In 2000 it was spotted off the Island of Sark, before making an appearance in Guernsey.

Alternative spellings of the name include, Griffin, Gryphon or Gryphin from the Latin word Gryphus.

Evolution of the Harp

The harp played an integral part in Celtic culture, particularly in Wales and Ireland, and continued to do so until the sixteenth century. The Harpists would often accompany their soldiers, leading them onto the battlefields, giving the men courage and spurring them on. In the sixteenth century however, the British crown banned the playing of this instrument in their attempt to control the ensuing uprisings and conflicts. The death penalty was issued, with the destruction of the harp. Despite its demise as an instrument, the harp remained a royal insignia, with Henry VIII using its form on the new currency, representing Ireland as part of his spreading kingdom.

With the birth of the United Irishmen in Belfast in 1791, the society of Irish Republicans adopted the harp as their crest and the Leinster flag representing the four provinces of Ireland and also featuring the harp, was used by them in 1798. The image of the harp continued to be used on currency, and it can still be found on the Irish euro today.

Evolution of the Lion

The lion has been greatly symbolic since the beginning of time; portrayed as the great hunter it was associated with kings but it was also the hunted, and representations of this beast appeared in hunting scenes depicted in mosaics on palace or mosque walls in some of the ancient Islamic countries. In India, the lion became symbolic of royalty more than 2000 years ago, as in certain parts of the country it was more widely hunted than the tiger.

Its image appeared on the ancient coinage of the Greeks, Egyptians and Romans, later being emulated by the Celts amongst others, and was represented in several different forms, sometimes appearing as just a roaring head or in rampant pose, and some examples depicted it attacking a bull. Ancient images of the mythological figure Hercules have represented him wearing a lion-skin headdress. In ancient Egypt, Amenhotep III built a temple guarded by two red granite lions, which were discovered by Lord Prudhoe on the Meroitic site of Gebel Barkal.

In religious representations of the lion, it appears notably with saints such as Jerome, who, in Bethlehem, had supposedly removed a thorn from the paw of such a creature, and was later portrayed with a lion in paintings by fifthteenth century artists such as Van der Weyden or Van Eyck. The lion was also emblematic of Saint Mark, and a winged representation of this animal, which was a common depiction during the Middle Ages can be found on one of the two columns of the Piazzetta, in Saint Mark's Square, Venice. Throughout Christianity, the lion continued to be symbolic, and examples of carved stone lions, particularly popular during the Victorian era, can still be found in cemeteries guarding the tombs against evil spirits, and notably representing 'resurrection'.

Pictish stone carvings often featured various forms of animal and an early example of this type of carving incorporating a lion was found in Kilduncan, Fife. The stone slab on one side revealed a wingless lion and two S-shaped sea creatures, possibly hippocampi, as well as an elaborately carved three-pointed triquera knot. The stone is currently on display at St Andrew's Museum, Fife.

During the earlier part of the Middle Ages, animals were often incorporated into heraldry, appearing on devices and charges, the most common being animals such as the stag, the dog, the boar, the martlet and the eagle. The lion was also still a widely used symbol, continuing to represent courage and bravery, and in Irish heraldry it could also be associated with a great warrior or chief.

In Scottish history, the lion is notably synonymous with King William, also referred to as 'William the Lion' whose battle standard was that of a red rampant lion on a yellow field, and who reigned as King of Scotland from 1143 to 1214. Despite being a fearless fighter, as a commander he lacked insight and was eventually taken prisoner by Henry II and held captive at his enemy's castle at Falaise, Normandy. A treaty, referred to as 'The Treaty of Falaise' was enforced by Henry, and the crippling taxes which ensued, which affected their economy, were endured by the Scots people for the following fifteen years. When Richard 'The Lion Heart' became the new King of England, in order to raise capital for his third crusade, he freed William from the treaty by selling him back his castles, which had remained in the possession of the British Crown; and so Scotland regained its independence once more. Even after his death, William's standard remained symbolic to the Scottish people and their independence.

The lion reappeared again in Scottish history, when King James VI, having succeeded Elizabeth to the throne, replaced one of the two unicorns supporting the shield on their Royal coat of arms, with a lion. This symbolic gesture was made during the time of the union between Scotland and England and has remained the official arms since. However, the old Scottish standard of 'William the Lion' still sometimes makes an unofficial appearance even today at events such as football or rugby matches.

Evolution of the Owl

The owl has been widely used as a symbol throughout history but is undoubtedly most synonymous with knowledge, learning and wisdom, with numerous references made to it, even in literature, including poems such as the one written by Edward Hersey Richards. It became particularly popular in the nineteenth century, especially in the United States with various universities or institutions such as the Smithsonian Institution, founded in 1835. The British founder James Smithson had bequeathed his estate to his nephew, who died without an heir. Smithson had stipulated that should this be the case, the estate would then be used to establish an institution in his name in Washington DC, for the increase and diffusion of knowledge amongst men. The institution was finally established as a trust in 1846, and it was the owl, which was chosen to represent their Smithsonian badge. The Royal College of General Practitioners founded in 1952, also incorporated the owl as part of their coat of arms. Other crests include Leeds Civic Council who have incorporated two owls supporting a shield and dates back to 1662, when the town was granted its Royal Charter. Football clubs such as Sheffield Wednesday, inspired by the district of Owlerton have used an owl on its club's crest. In Zimbabwe this bird has been used as an example of those Afro / European cultures sharing a symbol by appearing on the crest of an adult training college. In this instance the owl represents wisdom but in African culture in general it is associated with witchcraft. Owls have also appeared in statue form or incorporated into architecture, and the town of Dijon in France immortalized the owl in this way when their architect, who was believed to have been inspired by this bird, integrated it into the north wing of the parish of Notre Dame, making the owl symbolic of the town.

The owl however has also been depicted with negative connotations as it was regarded by the ancient Romans as a funerary bird, associated with the night and darkness and was a bad omen. To the ancient Egyptians it was symbolic of death. In some countries the owl is still surrounded by superstitions and viewed as a harbinger of death or misfortune, including Anglesey, Wales, where the barn owl is still associated in this way.

To the ancient Greeks, the owl was associated with the goddess, Athene, symbol of Athens, who represented not only certain attributes of war but also wisdom and the arts. Athene was frequently portrayed with an owl and there are still examples of fifth century coinage depicting her image or that of her owl. In Celtic civilization, both positive and negative aspects of the owl were symbolic.

There are an estimated 134 known species of owl and the oldest fossil remains are thought to be over 24 million years old. To date, there are approximately 3000 establishments that presently use or are still using the owl as its symbol.

Evolution of the Salmon

Some of the earliest examples of representations of the salmon, can be found on Pictish stone carvings, such as those found on the symbol stone 'Knowe O'Burrian', on display in the Orkney Museum, Kirkwall. In 1856, Dr J. Stuart, founder of 'The Spalding Club' in Aberdeen, illustrated copies of Pictish carved symbols, including the salmon, in his book the 'Sculptured Stones of Scotland'. In Garioch, Inverurie, Scotland, early settlers built sacred stone circles and farmed the land, a tradition which was continued by the Picts, who also carved images on the stones. In the River Don, at the Stanners, at its safest crossing point, they placed a symbolic stone in the water depicting a salmon and when its face was visible, only then was the ford safe to cross.

The Salmon continued to be a popular symbol into the Middle Ages, particularly with the Irish and the Scots, and appeared in certain heraldic devices or charges, representing clans. Clan heraldry could incorporate several symbols and at least four of the most notable symbols particular to the West Highlands were ones such as the galley, the rampant lion, the hand and the salmon. Clans such as the MacDonalds and the Macleans of Duart are just two examples featuring quartered arms incorporating the fish.

In Glasgow in 1270, the salmon was the first symbol to be portrayed on the seal of Bishop William Wyschard and was later followed by the bird, the tree and the bell. These were eventually represented together on the first seal, which is that of the Chapter of Glasgow, used between 1488-1540, and in 1647 were finally represented in their present form, but only becoming official in the nineteenth century. The two salmon are represented with a ring in each mouth and this depiction derives from the legend of 'Hydderech Haee', King of Cadzow. The Queen of Languoreth was given a ring as a present from the King but she gave it to her beloved knight, and whilst he lay sleeping, the King suspicious of his Queen, discovered the ring and stole it back. The King in fury, threw the ring into the River Clyde and on returning home, threatened the Queen with death if she failed to produce the gift. The knight confessed his sorry tale to Saint Mungo, who sent a monk in search of the ring, instructing him to bring back the first fish he caught. Saint Mungo fortuitously found the ring in the fish's mouth and returned it to the knight.

In Ireland, the town of Leixlip's name derives from its ancient Norse name of 'Lax-Hlaup' meaning 'salmon leap'. The town, which is situated near Dublin was an important Viking settlement and many battles were fought at Leixlip until Brian Boru, last great High King of Ireland won them their first real victory over the Nordic invaders in 1014 A.D. Located on the confluence of the Rivers Liffey and Rye, the river was rich in salmon and in 1734 the town's first tollhouse was built on the newly constructed bridge, charging a halfpenny to visitors arriving to witness the incredible sight of the salmon climbing the cataract. The town's crest incorporates a Viking long-ship and two leaping salmon.

The popularity of the salmon as a symbol has continued into the twentieth century with its depiction on the old Irish ten-pence piece; and it has also been represented on the Belfast waterfront in the form of a thirty-three feet long sculpture, known as the 'Big Fish', to celebrate the return of the salmon to their waters.

Evolution of the Snake

The image of the snake is most notably associated today with modern medicine, the symbol of the snake appearing entwined around a staff or rod. There are two represent-ations of this symbol, each depicted curled around the rod of Hermes, known as the caduceus or the staff of Aesculapius, who was the Roman god of medicine and a healer. In the latter context, a non-poisonous snake was represented as a therapeutic symbol, coiled around Aesculapius's healing staff. Hermes, the Roman Mercury, was the master of inventions and discoveries and was later associated with the arcane study of alchemy, with his rod therefore also becoming linked to that of Aesculapius and to the practice of medicine and chemistry in general. The renowned psychologist Carl Jung, believing in the snake's connection with both heaven and earth, adopted it as the symbolic emblem for homeopathic medicine.

The Americans adopted the snake too when Benjamin Franklin in 1751 retorted in a satirical commentary, that the American colonists should send by way of a thank you to the British, rattlesnakes in return for their convicted felons. Its symbolic image resurfaced again in 1765 in retaliation to the Stamp Act enforced by the British in their bid to gain further control over the colonies. In 1774 it was depicted fighting a British dragon in one newspaper caption and by 1775, the snake appeared on uniform buttons, flags, banners and paper money. Emblems eventually appeared, emblazoned with a fiercely coiled rattlesnake, with the slogan 'Don't Tread On Me' and became known as the Gadsden flag, becoming symbolic of American independence. The snake has always been symbolic to the Native American Indians, as they believe that their ancestors derive from animals.

Evolution of the Swastika

The swastika symbol was still being used in the Nordic

countries from 1000 AD onwards, often depicted on ancient runic stones, and its popularity as a geometric motif continued into the Middle Ages, incorporated in architecture as well as different forms of art. The pavement of the tallest cathedral in France, the Cathedral of Amiens constructed in the thirteenth century, retains a stunning example of this symbol in a repetitive black and white design.

Later in the nineteenth and twentieth centuries, other examples of this design could be found in the form of emblems and logos, particularly popular in countries such as Finland, where it was notably used by the military forces. In Sweden, the electrical machinery manufacturer, ASEA (now ABB) was also represented by the swastika. Robert Baden Powell used the symbol initially in the Boy Scouts movement in Britain, along with the writer Rudyard Kipling, who depicted the image of the swastika on the spines of his books, presumably denoting the original Hindu meaning, of 'good fortune'. It was also used in the same symbolic context by the 'Volkisch Nationalist Movements' in Germany, who were aware of its origins through the works of leading archaeologist, 'Heinrich Schliemann' after his discovery and subsequent research of the symbol, found on objects at the ancient site of Troy.

The use of the Swastika, with its positive connotations, was about to change when it appeared as the insignia for the Nazi Party in the early 1920's, at the time of Adolf Hitler's election as its chairman. Following the earlier conclusions of 'Schliemann' of its probable Indo-European origins, the Nazis associated their nation and the swastika's symbolism with that of the ancient Aryan peoples, believing them to be the original 'master race' or 'white invaders'. With Germany's radically changing reforms, the swastika soon became symbolic of what they eventually came to regard as their Aryan identity, and its use by others as a form of representation, almost gradually disappeared. The Hooked Cross as it was also referred to, was depicted on a black and red background, which supposedly represented blood and soil, and in 1935 was adopted as their national flag.

Despite its misappropriation by the Nazis and its subsequent negative image, the swastika has remained a symbol of 'good fortune' and 'well-being' in the Hindu culture.

Evolution of the Triskele / Triskelion

The image of the triskele is today perhaps most notably associated with Ireland, Brittany and the Isle of Man, and is still a symbol greatly linked with all that is Celtic. The Isle of Man, although originally regarded as a Druidic centre during early Celtic civilization, became more widely associated with the Vikings from around AD 700 when it was used as an outpost, until it came under the control of the Scottish Crown in the thirteenth Century.

The three-leg motif was depicted on tenth century runic crosses but became widely recognisable when it was represented on the Manx sword of state in the thirteenth century during the reign of King Olaf Godredson. The origins of the design of the three-leg symbol, were believed to have been influenced by the Island's Norse connections, and similarities have been remarked between their motif and that of the Valknut or Odins knot, which consists of three interlocked triangles. Its inspiration has also been attributed to the mythical god, 'Manannian Mac Lir', who in Manx legend, transformed himself one day into the form of three fiery legs, terrorizing the Viking invaders about to attack the Island. The design was altered however by Sir William le Scorpe, Lord of Man in 1395 and the three-leg symbol appeared featuring armoured legs. From the fourteenth century, the Island came under English jurisdiction, officially coming under the British Crown in 1765, and the flag was seldom used until the 1920's. Its final armoured and spurred design was established in 1966 and has been publicly recognised on the Island's flag since 1968, and the 'Ny Tree Cassyn' as it is also referred to, appears on their currency and number plates.

In 1847, the three-leg symbol became a popular trademark for Joseph Tyzack's Sheffield based tool manufacturers, as the result of a successful working relationship with the 'Isle of Man Steam Packet Company'. Inspired by the Isle of Man design, Joseph, nephew of William Tyzack, founder of the famous tool manufacturers, adopted the motif as its logo, and it still appears on the 'Tyzack Rapper Swords', which the company went on to produce and are still currently used in dancing.

Another country associated with the three-leg symbol, is Sicily, which in ancient history was also referred to as Trinacria due to its triangular form or three-cornered shape. In the Sicilian representation, the three-legs remain naked and are sometimes depicted with a head at the point where the thighs join. In 1808, during the period of the Napoleonic Empire and under the rule of Joachim Murat, the kingdom received new arms and the ancient symbol was once again revived.

In modern Brittany, the triskele has become emblematic of separatist movements such as 'Jeune Bretagne' or 'L'Alliance des Pays Celtes' and is a symbol, which has appeared in various representations and with varying degrees of significance. Other symbols sometimes associated with the Triskele are the Swastika and the Lauburu, the Basque cross, which consists of four comma or teardrop shaped heads and symbolizes prosperity.

GLOSSARY OF MYTHOLOGICAL CHARACTERS AND CELTIC TERMS

Aed Ruad / Aedh Ruadh: A King of Ireland who ruled in rotation every seven years with his cousins Cimbaeth and Dithorba. He was the father of Macha and was also referred to as 'Aed the Red'.

Arawen / Arawn: Lord of the Otherworld. He was a master hunter and possessed a pack of white hounds with red ears. Astride his white horse, he would hunt souls for the Otherworld. Associated with Welsh mythology.

Artio: Goddess associated with the bear and worshipped on the continent. She could represent the image of death and sometimes replaced the Druid god Dispater who was symbolic of night and death.

Arduinna / Arduiana: Goddess symbolic of the moon and hunting, and associated with the forest of the Ardennes. She was also attributed with the boar and other animals such as the bear. Arduiana was similar to the Roman goddess Diana. Associated with Gaul.

Bacchus: Roman god associated with intoxication, pleasure and plenty. He was attributed to the Thracian god of wine, Liber, and was notably identified with the grape and with harvest. Bacchus was symbolic of the arts and music and his festivals were renowned. He was sometimes depicted with the ram, possibly suggestive of fertility.

Badb / Badbh: Triple-war goddess, her name signifying 'fury'. She could take the form of a crow before battle, representing death; she could also appear in a grotesque form, which not only represented death but sexuality as well. Badb was notably associated with the goddesses, Nemhain, Macha and Morrigan.

Belenos / Bellonos / Belenus : Symbolic of healing and the light, his name signifying 'the shining one'. Associated with the Celtic festival Beltain or Beltene, he represented fire and purification. He was patron of the arts, and attributed to all that was beautiful and harmonious. Associated with Gaul.

Beltain / Beltene: This festival marked the end of the winter season and the beginning of summer. Celebrated on the first of May, the herds were returned to the hills, passing through bonfires for purification, presided over by the Druids. It was a celebration of light, warmth and new life associated with fertility, symbolic of planting and growth as well as the sun. The god Bellenos was symbolic with Beltain as was Lugh, both attributed with light.

Bladud: Prince Bladud, son of the Celtic King Lud. According to ancient legend, Bladud, afflicted with leprosy and exiled from his kingdom, became a swine herder. One day his infected herd, after wallowing in a muddy marsh, was cured. Bladud cured his affliction in the same way by bathing in the hot muddy water, which was in fact a healing spring. After returning home, where he eventually became King, he erected a temple by the spring as a mark of gratitude. The sacred spring situated on the outskirts of Bath, resulted in

Bladud's eventual association with the town.

Boand / Boand / Boanda: She was the wife of Elcmar, brother of Dagda, and was the spirit or goddess of the River Boyne. Her name also signified 'white cow'. In order to atone herself following her adultery with Dagda, she bathes in the water of Sagais but loses her arm, her leg and an eye. She fled to the sea in which she plunged to hide her disfigurement, which then became the River Boyne. She was sometimes known as Eithne. Ireland.

Bran: Known as 'Bran the Blessed' was associated with the crow and raven. Possessing the cauldron of abundance and regeneration, he was a master of life and death in the otherworld. Associated with Ireland.

Brid / Brighid / Brigid: Daughter of Dagda and one of the Great Mother triple goddesses of Ireland. Symbolic of fertility, healing, fire, poetry and prophecy, she was also the patron of craftsmen. Following the introduction of Christianity, she became known as Saint Brigit. Eventually due to her powers of healing, she became associated with wells and sacred springs.

Caer Ibormeith: In Irish mythology, she was a beautiful goddess of sleep and dreams, who was forced by her father to turn into the form of a swan every other year. She was the beloved of the god, Oengus.

Cairn: Ancient burial chamber. These tombs or burial chambers varied in size and construction and many of the examples found today are circular. Initially, the stone chamber was built, after which further stones were built up around it, creating a mound. Certain cairns, were constructed with passages or one long passage, allowing access from the outside to the chamber itself. Further studies have concluded that some of these chambers were visited repeatedly by the Druids or tribe members, possibly in connection with worship and sacred rituals. Ancestral worship was important and the burial of the dead was extremely symbolic. The 'Eagle Tomb' in the Orkneys discovered in 1958, contained the remains of 340 people. Other objects such as ceremonial tools, beads and bones as well as talons belonging to the white-tailed eagle were also discovered. The burial chamber of Newgrange, County Meath, Ireland is believed to pre-date Stonehenge and is regarded as the most significant of these sites known today. Remarkable examples of megalithic art can still be found carved into the stones, such as lozenge and geometric shapes as well as spirals, also in triple form.

Cernunnos: Lord of all animals and the god of nature. He was also referred to as the 'Horned God', due to his representation sometimes with antlers or horns. Symbolic of fertility and plenty, he is known to be one of the most ancient and important Celtic deities. His symbols include the horned serpent, the ram, the bull and the stag.

Conchobar: In Irish mythology, he was the son of the druid Cathbad and Nessa or Ness-Assa, a renowned warrior princess and daughter of the King of Ulster, Eochaid Salbuide. Later Conchobar became the King of Ulster and was associated with Cuchuainn in the Irish epics.

Cuchulainn / Setanta: The most important heroic warrior in

Irish mythology. Capable of good and bad, his character is associated with many of the great Irish epics. His brute force also gave him phallic connotations. He was also referred to as the 'Hound of Cualann'.

Daghda / Dagda: Supreme God and ruler of the Tuatha De Danann, Ireland. He was master of the people and father of the living and of the dead. He possessed three magical attributes, which were the harp, the club and the cauldron of abundance and regeneration.

Dana / Danu: In Ireland she was the Great Mother goddess of the Tuatha De Danann and was associated with certain birds such as the eagle, the falcon and the crow.

Derbforgaill: Daughter of King Lochlann Forgall, she could appear in the form of a swan. In search of Cuchulainn, whom she loved, he shot her down with his sling, wounding her. She then married Lugaid but died tragically and Lugaid himself died afterwards from grief. Associated with Ireland.

Elffin: It was Elffin the fisherman, who with his magic fishing net finds Taliesin who had been placed in a bag and thrown into the sea by his divine mother Keridwen. Elffin adopts the boy and takes care of him until he is thirteen years old. Wales.

Epona: Goddess of horses and protector of troops, she was associated with abundance and fertility, and was sometimes represented with fruit or the 'horn of plenty'. She was also attributed to the healing of domestic creatures and could be represented with various symbols including a bird, a dog or a foal. She also symbolized the safe passage of souls to the Otherworld. Associated with Gaul.

Esus: His name signified 'Master', representing earth's energies and forces, associated with creation. He was also the god of harvest, symbolic of fertility and prosperity. Esus was attributed to animals such as the crane and the bull but was equally linked to aspects of war. Associated with Gaul.

Fand: Wife of the sea-god, Manannan, she represented grace, and in Irish mythology she was also associated with Cuchulainn.

Finn / Fionn MacCumhail: Master of the animals of the forest and god of deer. He was the hero of the Fionne cycle in Irish mythology. It was Finn who first tasted the 'Salmon of Knowledge' caught by the druid Finnegas. After sucking his burnt thumb whilst cooking the fish, Finn ingested all the salmon's wisdom.

Flidias: Sylvan deity in Irish mythology, who ruled over the forest and wild animals. She was a shape-shifting spirit of the forest and drove around in a chariot drawn by deer. Flidias was similar to the Roman goddess of hunting, Diana.

Gwyon Bach: He was responsible for guarding the magic cauldron of Keridwen. After accidentally swallowing the three magic drops, which fell from the cauldron, Keridwen pursued him in fury, and eventually swallowed him when he transformed himself into a tiny grain of wheat. Gwyon Bach was later reborn as Taliesin. Wales.

Heracles / Hercules: Known in both Roman and Greek mythology. Renowned for his strength and virility he was attributed to the club and the lion-skin. According to Greek mythology, at the request of King Thespius, he impregnated the King's fifty daughters, thus demonstrating his virile and fertile powers.

Hermes: In Greek mythology he was a messenger from the gods to mortals, and was an orator, associated with writing. He also represented transition as well as boundaries. He was attributed to the sun and light, and his various symbols included the cockerel. Hermes was similar to the Roman god Mercury.

Janus: A Roman god worshipped at the beginning of harvest time and during the period of plantation. He was often associated with change and transition, symbolic of openings, beginnings and endings. Janus was notably depicted with two heads usually facing in opposite directions.

Jupiter: Roman god associated with the skies and regarded as one of the most powerful Roman deities.

Keridwen / Kerridwen: She was a magician, possessing the cauldron of inspiration, science and poets. She was the divine mother of Taliesin the Bard. Wales.

Lleu / Llew Llaw Gyffes: A renowned archer, his name signified 'Lleu of the steady hand' or 'lion of the steady hand'. His mother Arianrhod refused to name him and placed three maledictions on him: no name, no armour and that he would never marry. Upon his death, Lleu turned into an eagle.

Associated with Wales.

Libane / Liban: Sister of Fand, she was a goddess of love, pleasure and health, able to change herself into a swan. In Irish mythology, she was equally associated with druidism, witchcraft and the fairies, transforming herself partially into the form of a salmon.

Lug / Lugh: Supreme Celtic god, known under many different names. His name signified 'shining one' and he was a god of light and war. He possessed a magical harp and a magical lance or spear, and was often referred to as 'Lugh with the long arm'. Other symbols included the boar, the crow and the raven. Lug was the master over life and death, and equally the master of all arts, endowed with unlimited skills. He was a hero and a lord of the Tuatha De Danann. Lug was also represented as the 'god at the wheel' sometimes depicted in triple form or with three heads. Associated with Ireland and Gaul.

Macha: In Irish mythology she was a goddess of the Tuatha De Danaan and daughter of Aed Ruad. Symbolic of war and fertility, she was associated with Nemhain and Badb and could appear in the guise of a crow during battle. She possessed a triple aspect, ' the three or triple Macha' and was also known as 'Macha the red'.

Maelduin: Hero in Irish mythology, who made an epic journey by boat in search of his father's assassins. His perilous voyage was hampered by many obstacles, which he encountered on different islands.

Manannan Mac Lir: Irish Sea-God and son of Llyr, King of the Tuatha De Danann. He was associated with the sun and the horse, traversing the ocean in his chariot drawn by white horses. He transported souls to the Otherworld. The Isle Aran and Man were under his protection and the name of the latter reputedly derives from Mananann.

Medb: Associated with war, she was the warrior Queen of Connaught. Her name signified 'intoxication' and possessing the power to intoxicate, her look could remove the strength of men and she was able to outrun any horse. Medb is associated with the Irish epic 'Tain Bô Cualnge' also known as 'The Cattle Raid of Cooley'.

Morann: Judge and poet in Irish mythology. His symbol was a magical necklace.

Morgan / Morgane: A mother goddess who possessed many attributes, associated with the sea and also with death. Associated with the Arthurian epics and half-sister of Arthur, she nursed him back to life on the Island of Avalon where she lived with her seven sisters. Avalon was associated with the apple of immortality, knowledge and light. Associated with Ireland.

Morrigan / Morrigane: In Irish mythology she was a Triple Goddess, the Great Mother, the Crone and supreme goddess of war. She was a shape-shifter, associated with Badb and Macha or Nemhain and was attributed to the colour red, representing the warrior and the Otherworld. She was symbolic of death and fate, reigning over the battlefield with her crow-like cries. In Irish epics she formed part of the

'Morrigan triads'.

Mog Ruth / Mug Ruith: One of the most important druids in Irish mythology who was sometimes attributed to the sun. His breath could turn men to stone and he drove around in a chariot, which flew like a bird and shone like the sun. He was sometimes depicted wearing a bird mask. He was also referred to as the 'servant of the wheel'.

Nuada / Nudd: King of the Tuatha De Danaan who loses his right hand (or arm) in the battle of Mag Tured. Having lost his power as King, the god Dian Cecht fabricates Nuada a new hand made of silver, thus enabling him to regain his sovereignty. He became known as the 'King with the silver hand'. Associated with Ireland.

Oenghus / Aengus: Young god associated with love and beauty and son of Dagda in Irish mythology. He transformed himself into a swan to be reunited with his beautiful beloved Caer.

Ogham: Sacred writing of the Celts, known also as their tree alphabet. Its name derives from the god Ogma, its creator who kept its secret amongst the Tuatha De Danaan and the druids. The alphabet was notched onto wood or stone, with each of the twenty letters corresponding with the name of a tree symbolic to the druids. Ogham comprised of three sets of five consonants and one set of five vowels. Yew and hazel sticks were both symbolically attributed to this sacred writing, as they were reputedly used to make the notches.

Ogma: God and champion of the Tuatha De Danaan. As

champion, he represented great physical force and was associated with the club. He was equally the god of scholars and eloquence, referred to as 'the god of the golden speech' and was attributed to the sacred writing of ogham. He was also symbolic of inspiration, poetry and music. Associated with Ireland.

Osiris / Asar: Egyptian god of the Otherworld, associated with life and death. He was equally the god of vegetation, symbolizing the creative forces of nature and was notably depicted as a green man. His worship eventually spread into other cultures, including that of the Romans and Greeks.

Rhiannon: Great Queen and Mother-Goddess in Welsh mythology, attributed with horses and birds. She was symbolic of fertility and enchantment, possessing a totem of magical birds. Rhiannon was also associated with guiding souls to the Otherworld. She was the Welsh equivalent of Epona.

Samhain: The beginning of the New Year in Celtic tradition, pronouncing the seasonal changes, when darkness dominated the light, and the herds returned home from the fields. It marked the transitory stage symbolic of life and death not only associated with the end of the harvesting period but also life and death linked to the spiritual world. Communication with the spirits of the dead became possible during the period between October thirty-first and November first as the entrance to Otherworld opened. Communal fires were lit everywhere, protecting cattle and warding off evil spirits.

Sheela-na-gigs: Goddess of fertility, representing creation and destruction. Her image could notably be found above the doorways or arches of churches and sometimes castles, where she was depicted overtly displaying her genitalia. This depiction demonstrated her powerful sexual attributes symbolizing 'the all-consuming mother'. Her representation during Christianity could have signified flagrant lust or possibly that of protection. Many of her images can still be found today and there are believed to be around eighty, which still exist in their original location. Associated particularly with Ireland and Great Britain.

Sid / Sidh: Associated with the fairies in Irish mythology, it was a visible place associated with the Otherworld, symbolic of peace, and there were numerous references to the 'children or people of the Sidh'.

Stone of Fal / Lia Fail: Known also as the 'Stone of Destiny', it tands in one of the ring forts or 'Royal Seats' at Tara. In legend, the stone possessed magical powers and reputedly cried out its consent during the investiture of the rightful new King. The ancient standing stone is also considered to be symbolic of fertility.

Sulis/ Sul: Goddess of the sun as well as symbolic of healing. She was associated with springs and sacred wells, where her image could often be found. Sulis was often confused with the Roman goddess, Minerva, with whom she shared similar characteristics. She was associated with the healing waters of Bath. Associated with Great Britain and Gaul.

Taranis: God of thunder and lightning. As master of the skies, he was associated with the cosmic wheel and was sometimes represented with a serpent and an eagle. He was also attributed to the moon and the sun. Taranis was similar to Jupiter, Thor and Zeus. Associated with Gaul.

Tarvos Trigaranos: A bull-god sometimes represented with three cranes or herons on his back. He was symbolic of the unification of knowledge and turbulent forces. Associated with Gaul.

Taliesin: In Welsh mythology he was born and reborn, and was the divine son of Keridwen, and once Gwyon Bach, before being reborn as Taliesin. Possessing the gift of words, he became the master of Arthur's bards and was also a Druid as well as a prophet.

Tara: Dated as far back as the Neolithic period, the hill of Tara, in County Meath, Ireland was originally the 'Seat of the High Kings' and a centre sacred to the Druids. Once an Iron Age fortress comprising of two linked ring forts, it eventually became associated notably with religion, following the introduction of Christianity.

Teutates: Ancient and most powerful god of war, symbolic of protection, initiative and law. He was regarded as the 'father and ruler of the people' and was sometimes depicted plunging men into his cauldron, possibly symbolic of death or rejuvenation. Teutates was similar to the Roman god, Mars. Associated with Gaul.

Tuatha De Danaan: Name of the ancient people in Irish mythology, comprising gods, goddesses, druids and heroes who possessed great powers. They derived from Dana or Danu, the Great Mother goddess of all the ancient gods.

Twrch Trwyth / Twrch Henwen: The monstrous white boar or sow in Welsh mythology, associated with the Arthurian epics. It represented the spiritual power that Arthur desired but could not obtain. A fantastic chase ensues, however the sow still manages to escape Arthur in the end by throwing itself into the ocean.

BIBLIOGRAPHY

L'Univers des Celtes – Barry Cunliffe, Bilbliothèque de l'Image, 1993. Original title, The Celtic World - Barry Cunliffe, 1990.

Les Celtes – EDDL – Paris, 2001; (Gruppo Editoriale Fabbri Bompiani, Sonzogno, Etas S.p.A. Milano) – 1991.

L'Art Celtique – Unesco / Flammarion, 1990

Mystères Celtes, une religion de l'insaisissable – John Sharkey / Seuil, Editions du Seuil 1975. Original title, Celtic Mysteries, The Ancient Religion - Thames & Hudson, London, 1975.

L'Art Celte – Lloyd & Jennifer Laing, L'Univers de L'Art. Original title, Art of the Celts – Thames & Hudson, London, Paris, 1992.

Le Monde Irlandaise, Histoire et Civilisation du Peuple Irlandaise – Brian de Breffny, Am Albin Michel. Original Title, 'The Irish World'- Thames & Hudson, London, 1997.

Dictionnaire de Mythologie Celte – Jean-Paul Persigout, Editions du Rocher, 1985 & 1990.

La Tradition Celtique dans L'Art Roman – Marcel Moreau, Le Courrier du Livre, 1975.

La Religion des Celtes – Joseph Vendryes, Coop Breizh, 1997.

La Société Celtique – Françoise Le Roux, Christian-J. Guyonvarc'h, Editions Ouest-France Université, Rennes, 1991.

Les Fêtes Celtiques – Françoise Le Roux, Christian-J. Guyonvarc'h, Editions Ouest-France Université, Rennes, 1995.

Highlanders, Histoire des Clans d'Écosse – Fitzroy Maclean, Gallimard, France, 1995. David Campbell Publishers Ltd, 1995.

Dictionnaire des Symboles – Jean Chevalier & Alain Gheerbrant, Bouquins, Robert Laffont / Jupiter, 1982.

Ar Seiz Breur, 1923-1947, la creation Bretonne entre tradition et modernité – Terre de Brume, Musée de Bretagne, Rennes.

The Celts (New edition) – T.G.E. Powell, Thames & Hudson Ltd, London, 1958, 1980.

The Celts – Peter Berresford Ellis, Constable & Robinson Ltd, 2003.

The Artist & The Thinker, John Duncan & Patrick Geddes In Dundee – Edited by Matthew Jarron, The University of Dundee Museum Services, 2004.

Celtic Britain: Studies in Iconography and Tradition
– Anne Ross, Constable, London, 1992.

Celtic Britain – Charles Thomas, Thames & Hudson, London, New York, 1997.

Celtic Britain and Ireland – BCA, 1995.

The Illuminated Manuscript – Janet Backhouse, Phaidon Press, London, 1997.

Dictionary of Celtic Myth and Legend – Miranda Green, Thames & Hudson, London, New York, 1997.

Myths & Symbols in Pagan Europe – Hilda Ellis Davidson, Syracuse U.P. 1998.

Flags, coats of arms and badges of the Isle of Man – Michel R. Lupant, CEBED, 1996.

World Atlas of Flags – Whitney Smith / Brian Johnson Barker, New Holland Publishers, UK, 2004.

OTHER SOURCES OF INFORMATION

The Celts in Ancient History – T.W. Rolleston.

Symbols of Northern Ireland – University of Ulster, Ireland.

Institute of Irish Studies – Queens University Belfast, Ireland.

The Heraldry Society of Scotland, Edinburgh.

Smithsonian Institution, Washington DC.

Civic Heraldry of England & Scotland.

The National Trust, Devon & Cornwall.

University of Dundee, Museum Services, Scotland.

National Museums & Galleries of Wales.

Musée de Bretagne, Rennes, France.

Musée des Beaux-Arts, Quimper, France.

Musée Départemental Breton, Quimper, France.

ILLUSTRATIONS
SOURCES AND ACKNOWLEDGEMENTS

1. Wheel – detail from panel on the Gundestrup Cauldron
2. Horn – Bronze horned helmet, 1st c BC, England
3. Cauldron – Gundestrup Cauldron, silver, 3rd- 4th c BC, Denmark
4. Water - carved stone head, symbolic of sacred springs of Bath, England
5. Ram – detail from gold bracelet, 5th c, BC, Germany
6. Boat – Golden Boat, Broighter, 1st c BC, Ireland
7. Wolf – stone engraving, 7th c AD, Ardross, Scotland
8. Dog – based on dog taken from the Book of Kells
9. Fertility – Sheela-na-gig, stone carving from the medieval church of St Mary and St David, Kilpeck, Herefordshire, England
10. Head – double head (Janus) 2nd-3rd c BC, Roquepertuse, Bouches-du-Rhône, France
11. Cat – detail of head-mask with cats ears from bronze flagon, 5th c BC, Germany
12. Harp – the harp of the Irish King Brian Boru
13. Eagle – based on eagle taken from the Book of Armagh
14. Stone – sculpted four-sided pillar, 5th c BC, Germany
15. Stag / Deer – detail from sword sheath, 2nd c BC, La Tène, Switzerland
16. Torque – possibly 2nd c BC, Germany
17. Owl – detail from bronze cauldron, Denmark
18. Serpent – based on serpentine monster motif taken from a terracotta goblet, 5th c BC, France

19. Lance – lance-head 3rd – 4th c BC, Austria
20. Bull – bull's head taken from bronze cauldron, 3rd c BC, Denmark
21. Swastika – based on geometric motif on terracotta pitcher, 1st – 2nd c BC, Spain
22. Crow – based on bird illustration taken from the Book of Kells
23. Cranes – based on motif taken from armour, 1st c BC, Gaul
24. Heron – based on motif taken from iron helmet, 1st c BC, Yugoslavia
25. Sword – sword sheath engraving, 1st- 2nd c BC, Yugoslavia
26. Spiral – based on motif taken from the Book of Durrow
27. Triskele – Based on engraving on silver/gold cone, 8th c AD, Shetland Isles, Scotland
28. Swan/ water-bird – detail from bronze statue of goddess with helmet, 1st c AD
29. Horse – horse with rider in chariot on coin, 2nd c BC, Gaul
30. Bear – part of bronze statue of goddess Artio with bear, 2nd or 3rd c AD, Switzerland
31. Cockerel – small brooch or pin in form of cockerel, 4th – 5th c BC, Germany
32. Boar – bronze figurine, around 100 BC, Liechtenstein
33. Dragon – based on dragon motifs engraved on sword sheath, Hungary
34. Birds – based on bird-headed triskele, engraved on sword sheath, around 200 BC, Germany
35. Griffon – based on motif on griffon-headed vase, 7th c BC
36. Lion – detail from panel of the Gundestrup Cauldron

37. Cross – stone with cross carving of Fahan Mura, 9th c, Ireland
38. Numbers – Inspired by letter N taken from the Book of Durrow
39. Salmon - original design
40. Tree of Life – inspired by the Book of Kells
41. Butterfly – inspired by the Book of Kells
42. Celtic A – original design – apple
43. Celtic A (2) – original design – ash
44. Celtic Y – original design – yew
45. Celtic H – original design – hazel
46. Celtic O – original design – oak
47. Celtic M – original design – mistletoe
48. Club – original design
49. Celtic F – original design – fire
50. Patterns – based on various Celtic designs in the illuminated manuscripts
51. Trinity – based on varying representations of this symbol
52. Celtic C – original design representing symbol for colour
53. Wren – original design
54. Dove – original design
55. Circle – original design
56: Book Cover – inspired by the Book of Kells and various Celtic motifs

Artwork sources for The Evolution of Celtic symbols

Based on detail of Celtic motif taken from panel of wooden cabinet – by Joseph Savina, 1938 – part of the Ar Seiz Breur movement

Swastika motif – taken from the choir of the church of Notre Dame du Bourg, Rabastens, Tarn, France

Cockerel – based on current French rugby logo

Triskele – based on the three-legged version associated with Sicily, also known as the Trinacria

Snake – based on the Caduceus symbol associated with medicine, the Rod of Asclepius is usually represented with a wingless single snake

The publishers thank all museums and other holders of the various artefacts for their help. It is believed that the sources and acknowlegements given here are correct but if inadvertent errors have occurred please let us know and they will be rectified in later reprints and editions

NOTE: The illustrations in this book are representations of the original artefacts, which have been prepared as pencil drawings or as colour paintings by the author. In some cases the illustrations are original designs or paintings for which the author claims copyright.

HADLEY PAGER INFO PUBLICATIONS

Hadley Pager Info have been publishing books since 1996. Most publications are French-English and English-French Dictionaries, Glossaries and Phrasebooks of value to visitors and British residents in France and covering subjects as diverse as motoring, legal, gardening and horticulture, medical and health, building and renovation, veterinary and conversation in French. Details are given below.

Information on these and other forthcoming books can be found on our website www.hadleypager.com. Our books can be ordered through good bookshops in the UK, as well as through many internet bookshops or directly from us by sending details together with payment by cheque to Hadley Pager Info, PO Box 249, Leatherhead, KT23 3WX, England. (Books are post free within the UK but an extra charge is made for delivery outside the UK, see our website for details). Our current booklist is available on request through the above PO Box Number or by e-mail to hpinfo@aol.com

BILINGUAL PUBLICATIONS

All publications listed in this section are French-English and English-French

GLOSSARY OF HOUSE PURCHASE AND RENOVATION TERMS

Paperback, 2000, Fourth Edition, 56 pages, 210 x 148 mm
ISBN 978-1-872739-08-3   Price: £7.50

- Provides over 2000 French words and phrases used by estate agents, notaires, mortgage lenders, builders, decorators, etc.

GLOSSARY OF GARDENING AND HORTICULTURAL TERMS

Paperback, 2004, Third Edition, 72 pages, 210 x 148 mm
ISBN 978-1-872739-14-4   Price: £8.50
- The glossary includes nearly 2000 gardening and horticultural terms.
- The glossary matches up the familiar French and English names of pot and garden flowering plants and shrubs which are not readily available elsewhere.
- Lists Birds and Butterflies of France, also Medicinal Plants.

CONCISE DICTIONARY OF HOUSE BUILDING (Arranged by Trades)

Paperback, 2005, Third Edition, 304 pages, 210 x 144 mm
ISBN 978-1-872739-11-3   Price: £27.00

- Dictionary is divided into 14 sections covering the various stages and trades employed in house building: Architect, Earthworks and Foundations, Builder, Carpenter and Joiner, Woods and Veneers, Roofer, Ironmonger, Metals, Plumber, Glazier, Electrician, Plasterer, Painter and Decorator, Colours.
- Over 10.000 terms in each language. The book is the ideal companion when liaising with tradespeople or when visiting builders' merchants and DIY stores.

GLOSSARY OF FRENCH LEGAL TERMS

Paperback, 1999, 114 pages, 210 x 148 mm
ISBN 978-1-872739-07-6   Price: £12.00

- Provides over 4000 French legal words and phrases associated with legislation falling within the Civil Code and the Penal Code, (eg house purchase and wills), but company and commercial legislation is not covered.

HADLEY'S CONVERSATIONAL FRENCH PHRASE BOOK

Paperback, 1997, 256 pages, 148 x 105 mm
ISBN 978-1-872739-05-2   Price: £6.00

- Over 2000 French/English phrases and 2000 English/French phrases.
- Eleven conversational topic vocabularies.
- Aide-memoire key word dictionary.

CONVERSATIONAL FRENCH MADE EASY
By Monique Jackman

Paperback, 2005, 256 pages, 210 x 145 mm
ISBN 978-1-872739-15-1   Price £9.95

- Ideal for those with a basic knowledge of French who wish to improve and enhance their conversational skills. Particularly useful for those who have recently moved to France or have a second home there.
- The book covers some 120 French verbs with more than one meaning in French. The parallel French and English translations make working alone possible, or in pairs or groups of family members and friends.

HADLEY'S FRENCH MOTORING PHRASE BOOK & DICTIONARY

Paperback, 2001, 176 pages, 148 x 105 mm
ISBN 978-1-872739-09-0   Price: £6.00

- Asking the Way, Road Signs, Car Hire, Parking, Breakdowns, Accidents.
- Types of Vehicle, Cycling and Motor Sports.
- Extensive Dictionary Over 3000 words and phrases included.

GLOSSARY OF MEDICAL, HEALTH AND PHARMACY TERMS

Paperback, 2003, First Edition, 203 pages, 210 x 148 mm
ISBN 978-1-872739-12-0   Price: £12.50
- Provides over 3000 medical, health and pharmacy terms, including common illnesses and diseases, anatomical, first-aid and hospital terms.
- Brief aide-memoire definitions.
- Pharmacy terms include medicines, toiletries, cosmetics, health and pharmaceuticals.

HADLEY'S FRENCH MEDICAL PHRASE BOOK
By Susan Kirkham and Alan Lindsey

Paperback, 2004, 156 pages, 148 x 105 mm
ISBN 978-1-872739-13-7   Price £6.00

- Invaluable to travellers in France or in the UK seeking medical advice or medical treatment. Topics included are At the Doctor's, At the Hospital, Baby's, Children's, Young People's, Male and Female Health. Also At the Chemist's, At the Dentist, At the Optician's, Accidents and Emergencies.
- A Reference section is also included.

GLOSSARY OF VETERINARY TERMS
By Susan Kirkham

Paperback, 2006, 204 pages, 148 x 105 mm
ISBN 978-1-872739-17-5   Price £14.00
- Glossary of over 3000 Veterinary words and Phrases.
- At the Vet's.
- Pets' Passports.
- Invaluable for animal owners visiting or living in France.

OTHER PUBLICATIONS

SHERLOCK HOLMES AND A QUESTION OF SCIENCE
By Christopher Lindsey

Hardback, 2006, 208 pages, 240 x 170 mm
ISBN 978-1-872739-16-8   Price £ 12.50

- With its many illustrations , this is a book which will delight all fans of the Sherlock Holmes stories. It provides a fully researched and well-referenced account of the wide range of scientific knowledge and observation that Sherlock Holmes could bring to bear in solving the various murders and mysteries so eloquently developed by his creator Sir Arthur Conan Doyle.